VICTORIOUS PRAYING

ALAN REDPATH

VICTORIOUS PRAYING

STUDIES IN THE LORD'S PRAYER

Fleming H. Revell
A Division of Baker Book House Co
Grand Rapids, Michigan 49516

Published by Fleming H. Revell,
a division of Baker Book House Company
P.O. Box 6287, Grand Rapids, Michigan 49516-6287

ISBN: 0-8007-5489-1

Printed in the United States of America

Contents

Foreword

The contents of this book formed the subject of a series of messages given from the pulpit of Moody Memorial Church in the spring of 1954. I did not have in mind their publication, but, in answer to requests for this, I felt it might be in the will of God to share with a wider public some of the things that the Lord has been teaching me, and I trust showing others also, in the school of prayer in recent days.

There seems to be a tendency for many Christians to imagine that a church can be conducted and led in the same way as a business concern. Publicity, sales talk, propaganda, and a big front are all essentials in business, but the Church of Jesus Christ can only be led in blessing and power by men who have been humbled and broken at the cross, and who, through many experiences of their own failure and nothingness, have learned an utter dependence upon God, and have been taught by the Holy Spirit to lay hold of Him at the Throne of Grace. The Lord spoke to my own soul in the delivery of these messages based upon the Family Prayer, and I trust He may do so to everyone who reads this book.

My grateful thanks are due once again to Miss Arline Harris for her care and skill in the preparation of manuscripts.

ALAN REDPATH

The Moody Church
Chicago 14, Illinois

Victorious
Praying

Chapter I

Our Father Which Art in Heaven

We are going to turn in these chapters to an aspect of the Christian life upon which all other things depend, that is, our prayer life.

The experience of most of us when we pray, I feel, is rather like that of the man who was sick of the palsy. He and his four friends believed in the power and in the goodness of the Lord Jesus, but their problem was how to gain access to Him, how to reach His presence.

Is that not true of us today? How hard it is to get right through into the very presence of God when we pray! How difficult it is to force our way through the crowd of distracting thoughts, of worldly cares, even of sinful desires! For any of us who know anything at all of the school of prayer will know from experience that a man's holiest moments—at least the moments which should be his holiest—are the moments which are beset more than any others by the on-slaught of the enemy upon his mind and thoughts.

How hard it is to realize when we pray that God is, and that He is the rewarder of them that dili-gently seek Him! How seldom do we get through the clouds that seem to exist beneath His feet in order that we might, in prayer, see His face! Consequently, the prayer that is so often upon our lips and in our hearts is the request of the disciples: ". . . it came to pass, that, as Jesus was praying in a certain place, when he ceased, one of his disciples said unto him; Lord, teach us to pray . . ." (Luke 11:1).

It is not that we do not want to pray. It is rather that our experience in prayer often is such that we rise from our knees disappointed and frustrated, feeling that we have wasted our time in repeating meaningless worn-out phrases which somehow do not mean a great deal to us. When we have finished our praying, we can scarcely bring ourselves to be-lieve that our feeble words can have been heard, or that they can have made any difference in the things concerning which we have been praying. We've said our prayers, but we haven't prayed.

If we feel like that, how much more must the dis-ciples have felt it, who listened to the Lord Himself praying? When He had ceased, they pressed on Him the request, "Lord, teach us to pray." We can enter into their feeling of weakness, and we can also, thank God, share their comfort. For, like them, we can turn to Him and say, "Lord, teach us to pray."

To whom else could we turn that we might learn the secret? Who has the necessary gifts to answer that petition? What are the qualifications of the person who could instruct us in prayer? Surely the one who would teach us to pray must possess a perfect knowledge of the character and purpose of God. At the same time, he must have an equally perfect knowledge of the condition and plight of the human heart. He must know God perfectly and he must know us perfectly.

Therefore no one can teach us to pray like our Saviour. He has a perfect knowledge of the Father, for He was the outshining of the Father's glory, the express image of His substance. He said of Himself, ". . . he that hath seen me hath seen the Father. . . ."

Furthermore, He has a perfect knowledge of the human heart. He ". . . needed not that any should testify of man: for he knew what was in man," said John. He Himself is perfect man. His knowledge of our sorrows, of our temptations, of our problems, and of our needs, is absolutely perfect. For in visiting this dark world of ours, in entering our human life and in dying our death, He suffered as we suffer. ". . . we have not an high priest which cannot be touched with the feeling of our infirmities; but was in all points tempted like as we are, yet without sin" (Hebrews 4:15).

Our Saviour is the answer to the complaint of Job. In the midst of his trouble and suffering, faced with the misunderstanding of other people, Job com-

plained that there was no daysman, no umpire, none
who could lay his hand upon God, and at the same
time lay his hand upon man. Jesus is the One who
can touch the throne of heaven, and He is also the
One who can put underneath us the everlasting arms.
He knows God perfectly, and He knows you and me
perfectly.

He is the answer, not only to Job's complaint, but
also to his prayer, "Oh, that I knew where I might
find him! . . ." ". . . no man cometh unto the Father,
but by me," said the Lord Jesus. "Come unto me, all
ye that labour and are heavy laden, and I will give
you rest," for ". . . him that cometh to me I will in
no wise cast out."

We join with confidence and eagerness, and with
hungry hearts, this little group of men, as we gather
around the feet of the Saviour to cry, "Lord, teach
us to pray." And His answer is the same today as it
was then: "After this manner therefore pray ye: Our
Father which art in heaven . . ." (Matthew 6:9).

Whether you call this the "Lord's Prayer," or the
"Disciples' Prayer," or the "Family Prayer," doesn't
matter very much. It is not so much a form of prayer
as an example or pattern of the spirit of all praying
which is to be acceptable to God.

I am well aware, of course, that in some circles this
prayer is dispensed with altogether on the basis that
it is not for this Christian age of grace at all. At first
sight, and to the casual observer, there seems to be
little in it of Christianity. There seems to be nothing
in it of the Lord Jesus. There is no suggestion in it

that we are to pray to the Father in the name of the Son and in the power of the Holy Spirit, which surely is the avenue of all praying. Furthermore, there is no thought here apparently that we are forgiven by virtue of the blood; indeed, it suggests that we are forgiven on the basis of a meritorious act which we perform: we forgive others, then God will forgive us.

The fact is, however, that this prayer is full of the Lord Jesus Christ from beginning to end. Just as the Book of Esther, in which God is never mentioned, is full of God, this prayer in which the name of the Lord Jesus is never mentioned is full of Him. From the very first phrase of the prayer, where we must realize that it is impossible to come to God as our Father except we are born into His family through faith in Christ, to the very last word, the great "Amen," when we are reminded that the Lord Jesus is the great Amen of God, and all the promises of God are in Him "yea and amen"—right through this prayer, from beginning to end, we are in the presence of our Saviour.

We shall see this more clearly in succeeding chapters, and we shall also come to understand the significance of the teaching of this prayer concerning forgiveness as we study it phrase by phrase. My chief concern, however, is that we approach this prayer as the answer of Christ to the longing of all our hearts, "Lord, teach us to pray." If we do that, we cannot go very far before we meet the Lord Jesus in the pathway of this prayer, and find our hearts drawn out to Him in love as they have never been before. We cannot go far before we find the searching light of the Holy Spirit thrown upon us, and demands being made upon our lives which are utterly impossible to fulfill apart from the indwelling of the Holy Spirit.

Now look at the structure of this prayer as a whole. You will notice that it begins with worship: "Our Father which art in heaven, hallowed be Thy name"; it ends with praise: "For Thine is the kingdom, and the power, and the glory for ever, Amen." All true praying begins with the heart prostrate before God in adoration, and concludes in praise and thanksgiving with assurance that God has heard and answered us.

The simplicity of this prayer is such that parents can kneel down beside their children and teach them to utter its phrases. It is indeed so simple that a little child can understand it, yet so profound that its depths are unfathomable though a scholar spend a lifetime in the study of it. Maybe the problem with many of us is that we have ceased to be children in our prayer life and we make it too complicated.

As to theology, this prayer destroys every false and unworthy conception of God. As a principle of life, this prayer ushers a man into an experience of deliverance from sin. As a basis for social relationship it lays the only foundation for human fellowship throughout the world. As a prophecy it reveals the world as it is now, which one day is to be transformed into the kingdom of God, in which the will of God is done on earth as it is in heaven. It foretells the deliverance of all the people of God from every form of sin and evil.

In the second place, notice not only the structure of this prayer but its sequence, the melody as well as the harmony of it. There are seven requests mentioned here, divided into two categories. The first part contains three petitions concerning God, and the second contains four petitions concerning ourselves.

Listen to these: "Hallowed be Thy name. . . . Thy kingdom come. . . . Thy will be done." Here we have *Thy* name, *Thy* kingdom, and *Thy* will. A man learning how to pray is being taught here, first of all, to put the glory of God before everything. Thy name, Lord! Thy kingdom, Lord! Thy will, Lord! And then: "Give *us* our daily bread . . . forgive *us* our sins, our debts . . . lead *us* not into temptation . . . deliver *us* from evil"—our food, our sins, temptation, evil.

Christian friends, is it necessary for me to stress that in all true prayer the glory of God has to come before the need of our heart? I think it is, because so often you and I reverse the process. How we hurry into the presence of God and pour out to Him the story of our wants, our troubles, our temptations! Perhaps then we take just a minute, when we've finished with all that, to ask for His glory, or add a postscript concerning that missionary in Africa who comes to our mind. How this pattern of prayer given by our Lord shows up all that kind of praying!

First of all come *His* will, *His* glory, *His* kingdom, and then our needs. Why should that be? Is it (forgive the irreverence) apparent selfishness on God's part? Oh, no! The object of all true praying, you see, is not to bend the will of God to mine, but to get my will in line with His. True praying is not overcoming God's reluctance but laying hold of His willingness. Real prayer does not begin by attempting to persuade God to do something contrary to His will, but starts with worship and adoration, the prostration of my heart and spirit before the throne in utter surrender. ". . . seek ye first the kingdom of God, and His righteousness; and all these things shall be added unto you" (Matthew 6:33).

Prayer is not primarily a means of getting something done, it is a concern for the glory of God.

Every Sunday we receive in my church a number of requests for prayer. We count it a privilege to be entrusted with these and seek to enter sympathetically into every prayer request with the one who has sought prayer for his needs. Is it not, however, a reflection upon the general standard of our praying that practically all of these requests center around physical needs? Very seldom do we get a request to pray for a real spiritual issue, a revelation of the will of God, the glory of God in the life, the breaking through of the power of God in hearts.

The deepest need of an assembly of God's people as they worship is not that God would touch their bodies, but that He would break into their hearts by His Holy Spirit. The need in every church, Sunday by Sunday, in answer to the prayer of the Lord's people, is for a revelation of the glory of the Lord in the midst, that every church auditorium should pulsate with heavenly light, and that every visitor should sense that God is there! The purpose of prayer in a church service is publicly to seek first the kingdom of God, to put His name before everything else and His will uppermost, to worship Him and *then* to intercede on behalf of the needs of other people.

See again in this sequence of the Lord's Prayer the striking contrast between the two parts of it. In the first part, concerning these three petitions relating to God, notice that the prayer moves from within to without: from the inward shrine of worship to the outward place of service: "Our Father which art in heaven . . . Thy will be done in earth." In the second part of the prayer, concerning the need of the human heart, observe that the prayer moves from without to within, from the outward need of bread to the inward place of spiritual conflict: "Give us day by day our daily bread . . . deliver us from evil." In the first part of the prayer God moves from heaven to earth; in the second part of the prayer we move from earth to heaven.

Halfway we meet through the blood of Jesus Christ, for the very central theme of the prayer, the very phrase that stands right out in the heart of it is "Lord, forgive us our debts." God moves earthward from heaven; man moves heavenward from earth, and we meet in the very heart of this prayer on the only basis that any man can meet with God, the blood of the cross. The greatest need of every human heart as we seek the face of our Father in heaven is for His forgiving love and His redeeming mercy.

This prayer, therefore, is full of movement, full of activity: it is God acting and the heart of man responding. Heavenly spiritual forces move down to meet our need; the cry of the human heart rises from the depths to the throne.

Finally, in this chapter, let us consider the first sentence of this prayer: "Our Father which art in heaven." Notice that when we pray we begin with His name, and then we say, "Thy will be done." If you reverse that order, you pray to a God you do not know, and to accept the will of such a God would be slavery and sullen submission. But to begin with His name, to know God as your Father, and then to surrender to His will is a glad expression of the love of our hearts. The slave becomes a child—"Our Father."

It is the Saviour who teaches us to call God our Father, and this name of God signifies His character. If we call Him "Father," therefore, we are in His family. God is the father of all men only in the sense in which He is the creator of all men. The true relationship of father and son is dependent upon birth into the family. ". . . ye are all the children of God," says Paul to the church at Galatia, "by faith in Christ Jesus." You can only call God your Father in that sense if you are born into the family through receiving the Lord Jesus Christ as your own Saviour.

If God is our Father apart from that relationship He still has the right to claim our submission and obedience: ". . . thou shalt love the Lord thy God with all thy heart, and with all thy soul, with all thy mind, and with all thy strength, . . ." was the basis of human relationship to God apart from Jesus Christ. But we dare not claim relationship on that basis because we could not possibly fulfill its obligations. The Lord Christ alone is the true Son of God who can call Him "Father." He is the only begotten of the Father, the Word who is God made flesh, and through Him we have received the spirit of adoption. Having been adopted into the family circle, we can look up to the throne and say with Jesus Christ, "Our Father."

Yes, this is a family prayer, and that is what I like most of all to call it. It is based on relationship with God through faith in Christ, and only those who are in the family can breathe it.

Then notice that He is "Our Father which art in *heaven*." The correct translation is, "which art *in the heavens*." The New Testament speaks of three heavens: "the birds of the heaven," which obviously refers to the air surrounding the earth; and the "wonders of the heavens," which are the sun, moon, and stars. Then Paul speaks of being caught up into "the third heaven." Oh, my friend, God is in them all! "Our Father which art *in the heavens*." He is in the heavens far above our comprehension and understanding, but He is also in the very air we breathe.

He is in the glory, in the place where world tumult and world suffering and world conflict are never felt, except with compassion. He is away from the place of conflict, away from the stress and strain, in the place of authority and peace and truth. But He is closer than hands and feet and nearer than breathing —"Our Father!"

Have you noticed the possessives of this prayer, and how often the personal pronouns occur? "Give *us* this day *our* daily bread . . . forgive *us our* debts . . . lead *us* not into temptation . . . deliver *us* from evil."

This indicates a man alone with God with the whole world on his heart, a man in solitude with the door shut, with even his family on the other side. But although he is alone, on his heart is his family, his little ones, his home circle, his church, his friends, his whole world—the whole prodigal world for which Jesus died.

"Our Father!" All true prayer begins when I claim my relationship and become conscious of the responsibility which arises out of it.

It is said that the only child is the spoiled child. But it doesn't necessarily follow: an only child can be very precious, and the subject of wise discipline. However, you are not an only child in God's family, my friend, for He is *our* Father! I'm afraid that so often we ask in prayer as if we were an only child, and we become peevish and cross and resentful. Don't behave like a spoiled child when you pray! I am bound up in a bundle of life with the Lord my God, but with all of you as well, and with every born-again child of God throughout the whole world, no matter what his color. Some are only just beginning to learn to lisp the prayer. Some are on the verge of that great and glorious hour when they come into the presence of the God they have loved and served. Some are just little children who have learned to love the Lord Jesus. Some are mature men in faith. But to us all He is "Our Father."

If that is true, what tender relationship there should be between those in His family, shouldn't there? If I am harsh, or surly, or unforgiving, or critical, or resentful, or unkind to my brethren, how can I kneel before God and say, "Our Father"! Of course, though I be unkind to others and though I treat my brethren as I ought not, He is still my Father. But if I do that, His face is turned away from me.

What an unhappy time it is in the home when a little child needs correction and has to be punished! I remember wilting under the pressure of a good stout cane many times and walking very delicately for a few days. My father would say to me, "My dear boy, this hurts me more than it does you." I never believed that then, but I do now! I know the pain of a father's heart. The pain the child suffers is physical; the pain the father suffers is deep down with a wounded spirit. But all the time of that discipline, when the child is sent to his or her room alone, though he is being punished, he is still my child. The relationship has not been touched, although the fellowship has been broken because of his disobedience. In his peevishness and fretfulness my face has been turned away, and I am hurt and grieved. But there comes a moment (and oh, what a moment!) when that little one says, "Daddy, I'm sorry." Hardly are the words out of his mouth before Daddy's arms are around him, the fellowship is restored, and the home is filled with singing and laughter and joy and happiness. The cloud is gone!

God is our Father and we are His children. Has His face been turned away? Come to Him now and say, "Lord Jesus, I'm sorry." He always has His arms outstretched to welcome His wayward children. Then thank Him for cleansing and forgiveness, and sing:

> My Jesus, I love Thee, I know Thou art mine;
> For Thee all the follies of sin I resign.
> My gracious Redeemer, My Saviour art Thou;
> If ever I loved Thee, My Jesus, 'tis now.

Chapter II

Hallowed Be Thy Name

In our opening study of this pattern of all true prayer, we saw that it begins by claiming our relationship with God. No one can pray until he can say, "Our Father," that is, until he has come to know Him through faith in Jesus Christ and has been born into the family of God.

The revelation to our souls of the truth that the Great Creator is our Father brings us before His face in reverent worship. Therefore it is not surprising that the very next sentence in the family prayer is "Hallowed be Thy name." True worship of God is always followed by a deep concern for His glory.

This phrase contains the first of seven petitions in the Lord's prayer. We have already seen that four of them concern our needs and three of them concern God. These three take priority. The fundamental conception, the first concern, the primary desire of all our praying is "Hallowed be Thy name." It is this phrase upon which I want to meditate for a little while with you. We will consider what this petition involves and how we may see it answered in our own lives.

In the first place, the name of God is hallowed by divine revelation. Paul said, ". . . the invisible things of him from the creation of the world are clearly seen, being understood by the things that are made, even his eternal power and Godhead . . ." (Romans 1:20). Certainly the glory of God is revealed in all His creation. "The heavens declare the glory of God," sang the Psalmist, "and the firmament showeth his handiwork" (Psalm 19:1). I wonder if you know these lovely lines which are very precious to me,

> If Thy works praise Thee, Giver of good,
> If the sun shines its praise unto Thee,
> If the wind, as it sighs through the wood,
> Makes a murmur of song from each tree;
> Then these lips, sure, a tribute would bring,
> Though unworthy their praises may be;
> Shall all nature be vocal and sing,
> And no psalm of rejoicing from me?

But to get nearer to our subject: in the Word of God the name of God is always an expression of His character. He was known to His people in Old Testament days as Jehovah, "I am that I am," or more literally, "I will become whatsoever I please." More literally still, I believe that the Hebrew word, YAVAH, can be translated "the Becoming One"—the God whose purposes are sure, whose will is sovereign, whose word is irrevocable—Jehovah.

As the years passed by, many variations of that name were given and used by God's people. Sometimes it was Jehovah-jireh, "the Lord will provide," or "the Lord doth see." By that name Abraham came to know Him on Mount Moriah when he offered up Isaac in utter, complete obedience to the will of God. There God provided the lamb for the burnt offering in Isaac's place.

Sometimes He was known as Jehovah-nissi, "the Lord our banner." By that name Moses called Him one day when down in the valley there was warfare between Amalek and Israel. As Moses lifted up his hands to God in prayer, the tide of battle turned and Amalek was defeated. Moses raised an altar to the Lord there and called it Jehovah-nissi, "the Lord our banner."

He also became known as Jehovah-Shalom, "the Lord our peace." When God spoke to Gideon and called him from his daily tasks to a place of leadership for which he felt utterly unworthy, a place of responsibility which he felt to be far too great for him, Gideon raised an altar to the Lord and called Him Jehovah-Shalom, "the Lord my peace."

Sometimes He was known as Jehovah-tsidkenu, "the Lord our righteousness." By that name He revealed Himself to Jeremiah in the days of captivity when everything was going against the people of God, in days when they were in bondage. The outlook seemed grim indeed. But He revealed Himself at that time of bitterness and trouble as the One who would come one day and establish in this world His justice and His judgment, "the Lord our righteousness."

There are many other names by which His people came to know Him, all revealing the character of the God whom they worshiped, all of them centering upon Him as Jehovah, the omnipotent Almighty God.

But now I bring you to the day when He came Himself in human form to share our sorrows and trials, He who was holy, harmless, separate, undefiled. Yet He brought strength to the weak; He cleansed the leper; He raised the dead; He forgave the sinner. As He came to the end of those thirty-three years, He said, "I have manifested thy name. . . ." In other words He said, "I have revealed Thyself; I have declared Thy character; I have hallowed Thy name to those whom Thou hast given me out of the world."

The name of God is supremely and finally revealed in Jesus Christ. If we think for one moment of that place called Calvary, we know that it needs no words of His from that cross to tell us of the character of God. For if we stop and think about that cross, and we see our Saviour shedding His blood there, then we know God's estimate of our sins. We know that He hates our sin so greatly that He required the death of His Son that it might be put away.

We have but to think upon His cross to know that although God hates our sin, yet He loves us.

Yes, God loves us so unfailingly and unchangingly that He cannot allow us to go on in sin, and ultimately into hell, except He provide the way of deliverance and salvation. I know that God was in Christ reconciling the world to Himself, and that while we were yet sinners Christ died for us. I know that God is holy, infinitely holy, and that our sin must be punished but I also know that God is love, absolute love, and He longs to save us. As I gaze upon a cross "outside a city wall," I understand something of the character of God.

"I have manifested thy name . . . ," said Jesus, and He did it supremely when He hung between two thieves, bearing our guilt and shame.

That is not all, however, for today this same God speaks in the plainest of language to His children by His Holy Spirit. We say that God is with us when we meet in His presence, that where two or three are met together in His name He is in the midst. Where is He? We say that when we come to worship we meet with Him, for He is there. Where is He? He does not float in the atmosphere! He is incarnate in the personality of every born-again man and woman bowed in His presence—nowhere else!

He is with you in the power of the Holy Spirit that He might reveal Himself to you and speak with that still small voice, and that He may make real in your experience all that Jesus revealed the Father to be in His life. ". . . God . . . hath shined in our hearts, to give the light of the knowledge of the glory of God in the face of Jesus Christ" (II Corinthians 4:6).

That same God is Jehovah-jireh, the Lord who sees, the Lord who knows, the Lord who understands, the

Lord who provides. He is with us today as Jehovah-nissi, the Lord my victory, the Lord my banner in the fight, the Lord in whose power I can conquer. He is Jehovah-Shalom, the Lord my peace, the Lord my calm, my tranquility, my serenity, my deep peace. He is also Jehovah-tsidkenu, the Lord my righteousness. All-conscious though we may be of our unworthiness, we stand in the presence of God clothed in the righteousness of His Son, accepted in the Beloved.

His name, His character, is hallowed by revelation: Father, Son and Holy Spirit revealing their character to us today supremely in the Lord Jesus Christ, and seeking to make that character become real in our lives—"Hallowed be Thy name."

His name is hallowed not only by revelation, but His name is hallowed when we honor our relationship with Him. Really to pray, "Hallowed be Thy name," is to pray at the deepest level of which any man or woman is capable. For it means that, first and foremost, I desire in my life and through my life to others to reveal the name of Jesus and the character of God. I am therefore supremely concerned that every detail of my life should be for His glory. In other words, because I can look up into His face and call Him "Father," because I understand something of the character of the God I worship, I desire to honor that relationship by so living that I might be worthy of it.

As a Christian worker and as a servant of God this concern will be uppermost in everything I do in the Master's name. Whatever service you or I may undertake, our first thought in it all will be, "Is this for His glory?" Can I write "Hallowed be Thy name" over that program that I have planned for Him? Is it, in every detail, designed to bring glory to the Lord Jesus Christ?

This thought will be uppermost in choosing the books that I read. Over all my library can it be written, "Hallowed be Thy name"? If not, any bit of literature, any book over which I cannot write that will be cast out and burned in the fire; I will see to it that my book shelf bears "Hallowed be Thy name."

This phrase applies to the friends that I make, and how I treat them. I shall see to it that over every friendship and association, over every human affection and every human love, in the way I treat my friends and associates, the way I deal with the opposite sex—over it all will be written, "Hallowed be Thy name." Every relationship in life over which I cannot write it will be stopped at once, or else I can never pray this prayer again.

It will be my chief concern in all the habits that I form and all the ambitions that I cherish. If I find myself a slave to a habit, or impelled by ambitions over which I cannot write, "Hallowed be Thy name" then, by the help and power of God—Jehovah-nissi, the Lord my victory—it will be cast out.

This will be my supreme object in every pleasure that I seek, and if I discover my heart being wooed by material things, by fleshly desires, and by unworthy amusements, then they will be stopped. If I find myself staying by my television when I ought to be at the prayer meeting, I cannot pray, "Hallowed be Thy name."

This will be my attitude concerning every sorrow and trial through which, in the purpose of God, He may please to lead His child. I will seek to understand the meaning of it to the glory of God. In the midst of trouble and suffering and trials which may seem too great to bear, I will bow to the sovereignty of God and thank Him that in it all I can look up to Him and say, "Lord, above everything else, whatever may happen, hallowed be Thy name!" To think and to pray along these lines somehow puts a new dignity into life. It brings a new radiance into our character and a new reverence into our worship. Surely nothing in all the world today is needed more than that His children should be able to pray with sincerity, "Hallowed be Thy name."

Do we desire above everything that He should be to us Jehovah-jireh, the Lord who provides, the Lord who sees and understands? Do we desire Him to be Jehovah-nissi, the Lord my victory in every situation? Do we long that He might be Jehovah-Shalom, the Lord my peace, keeping us in tranquility and quietness? Do we desire that He should be to us Jehovah-tsidkenu, the Lord my righteousness? Then if we truly want these things, and say, "Hallowed be Thy name," we will first and foremost seek to honor our relationship to Him, for His name is hallowed when we do so.

But one other thing I must say here about this phrase of the Lord's prayer, and it is very important.

His name is hallowed by human recognition. As Jesus revealed the Father, so we are here to reveal Christ. I know of no reason why God does not take His children straight into heaven immediately they are born again except that He purposes that through us His name shall be revealed.

What a challenging word the Apostle Paul uttered to the Jews of his day when he wrote in Romans 2:24, ". . . the name of God is blasphemed among the Gentiles because of you"! It is a solemn thought to realize that failure on your part and mine to hallow the name of the Lord has disastrous consequences, for it causes that name to be blasphemed by others. It is strange that the world expects such a high level of living from those of us who name the name of Jesus —sometimes they put up a higher standard for Christianity than we are prepared to accept for ourselves.

Therefore, because it is true that over and over again carelessness in conduct, carelessness in speech, carelessness in life and discipline bring shame upon His name, I ask you what value it is to repeat in the house of God on Sunday "Hallowed be Thy name," if we are responsible for that name being dishonored in office and home during the week? What value is there in coming piously to pray, "Lord, hallowed be Thy name," and then to drag it down by our conduct the other six days?

To pray that prayer means it is our hearts' desire in bearing the name of Christ that others may see His character expressed in our lives. I believe there ought to be infinitely more of kindness, of charity, of endurance, of loyalty, of sacrifice, of love, in the lives of Christian people, far beyond anything in the lives of others. It is tragic that so often these qualities of grace are missing in Christians.

Because He is Jehovah-jireh, "God will provide"; because He will make all His mountains a way, therefore my behavior in the crises of life should glorify the name of Jesus Christ.

Because He is Jehovah-nissi, "God my victory," others should see a victorious life being lived out through me which is quite beyond human explanation.

Because He is Jehovah-Shalom, "God my peace," others should observe in your life and mine a tranquility and calm, a freedom from confused hurry and panic, a steadiness, a poise, a calmness, a sweetness, a peace which is outside human comprehension.

Because He is Jehovah-tsidkenu, "God my righteousness," others should observe in your life and mine a high standard: integrity of conduct, honesty of purpose, truthfulness which neither exaggerates nor minimizes. In all our dealings with others there should be something that can only be explained by the fact that it is no longer we who live, but Christ who lives in us.

What sort of mirrors are we to reflect His name? Is that reflection of Christ marred by sin, spoiled by our absorption in lesser things? Is it dimmed because in some aspects of life I do not honor my relationship with my Father in heaven?

There are hungry hearts who will never realize their need because they do not know what it is they desire until one day they see the Lord Jesus in you. It is that incarnate revelation of Jesus Christ in the life of a Christian which makes men and women thirst after God, for it crystallizes the thing that they have been seeking and cannot express. It meets the need of the heart which is burdened and lonely and troubled and does not know the answer. The moment they see a child of God who hallows the name of God, at that moment they see one who possesses what they need. Oh, that His name might be hallowed, that Father-relationship honored, that Christ-image recognized, so that the very life you and I live in ordinary surroundings may be so clear and transparent that it will bring others face to face with reality!

> Fill Thou my life, O Lord my God,
>   In every part with praise,
> That my whole being may proclaim
>   Thy being and Thy ways.
> Not for the lip of praise alone,
>   Nor e'en the praising heart
> I ask, but for a life made up
>   Of praise in every part.
>
> So shall each fear, each fret, each care
>   Be turned into a song,
> And every winding of the way
>   The echo shall prolong:

So shall no part of day or night
From sacredness be free:
But all my life, in every step,
Be fellowship with Thee.

—Horatio Bonar

Chapter III

Thy Kingdom Come

It is not unnatural that this prayer which begins in the inner shrine of the worship of God should move out into missionary zeal and concern for the glory of God. The moment we really pray, "Our Father which art in heaven," and realize something of the blessedness and joy of that relationship, our first concern is that others might share that relationship and enter with us into the kingdom of God. "Thy kingdom come" is always the desire of the heart which has entered into relationship with God and is eager that others should come into that joy also.

"Hallowed be Thy name" is a cry of adoration. The moment we really do express concern for the glory of God and have a real desire that in every detail

of our lives He should be glorified, we become absolutely convinced of our inability to glorify Him unless first of all His kingdom be established in our
hearts.

We find in "Thy kingdom come," therefore, a two-
fold meaning: it anticipates a kingdom of glory, and
prays for a kingdom of grace. The first is prophetic
and anticipates the future; the second is personal and
claims an experience today. This petition takes the
whole world in its scope as it looks forward to the
fulfillment of all the promises of God in Jesus Christ.
But it is also intensely personal: "O God, Thy kingdom come in my life!" For none can pray, "Thy
kingdom come in the world" until first they have
prayed, "Thy kingdom come in my heart."

I want to ask you to think with me about this two-
fold aspect of the "Family Prayer"—the kingdom of
glory which is prophetic, and the kingdom of grace
which is personal. And then we will have something
to say in conclusion about the practical implications
of this in our lives.

In his book on this prayer, *After This Manner*, Dr.
J. C. Macaulay has this trenchant phrase: "The
humanistic optimism which ushered in the twentieth
century lies buried amid the rubble of two world
wars and in the feverish preparations for a third,
which promises to make the first two look like mere
skirmishes." It is against that very serious, urgent
background that the people of God throughout the
world pray, "Thy kingdom come."

But not all of them mean the same thing when they

utter that prayer. What do we mean when we pray, "Thy kingdom come"? Do we mean that the kingdom of God is going to be established upon this earth? Yes, we do! Do we mean it will be established gradually by human effort and endeavor coupled, of course, with Christian activity and missionary enterprise, and that the world will gradually be changed and evolved into the kingdom of God? No, we do not!

The Word of God leaves no possible doubt to the open-minded reader concerning this subject. It declares that Christ Himself shall come before—and not after—a reign of righteousness and peace has been established upon the earth. He will come, not because these things have been accomplished, but in order that He might accomplish them, and that is a very different thing. In Isaiah 9:6-7 we read, ". . . the government shall be upon his shoulder. . . . Of the increase of his government and peace there shall be no end, upon the throne of David, and upon his kingdom, to order it, and to establish it with judgment and with justice from henceforth even for ever. The zeal of the Lord of hosts will perform this."

Again, the Spirit of God speaking through Daniel as he sought to interpret that remarkable dream of Nebuchadnezzar, who had seen a colossus of world power and observed how "a stone cut out without hands" crashed into the image and brought it down into dust: "This," said Daniel concerning it, "is the kingdom which the God of heaven shall set up, which shall break in pieces and consume all these kingdoms, and it shall stand for ever" (Daniel 2:44).

In the fullness of time, when Gabriel announced to the Virgin Mary the child which was to be born to her, he said, "He shall be great, and shall be called the Son of the Highest: the Lord God shall give unto him the throne of his father David: And he shall reign over the house of Jacob for ever; and of his kingdom there shall be no end" (Luke 1:32-33). The Lord Jesus Christ Himself said, "When the Son of man shall come in his glory, and all the holy angels with him, then shall he sit upon the throne of his glory" (Matthew 25:31).

These and many other passages in the Word of God deal with His kingdom that will come, and, my friend, when you pray, "Thy kingdom come," you pray for the fulfillment of all God's purposes on earth. You cannot pray this prayer as a mere form or ritual. When your heart goes out to the Lord in prayer and you say, "O God, Thy kingdom come," you are echoing the desire of all creation, you are repeating the song around the throne of God in heaven, and you are sharing the burden even of the Father Himself.

For it is here in this world in which we live where God will one day reveal His glory. It is here on this earth where Jesus Christ is to be King. It is here where He was born, where He lived, where He suffered, and where He was crucified—it is here that He shall reign. Therefore it is a very misleading statement for anyone to suggest that this world will disappear by hydrogen bombs. I do not mean that we may not have such atrocities inflicted upon us, but I do believe that Jesus will come and stop it! For this

world which has known the sweat and blood, toil
and tears of the Man of Sorrows soon will taste the
glory of His reign. Such a thing will not come gradually, but will be accomplished by divine intervention.
Indeed, how else could it be accomplished?

Today Satan is the prince of this world, blinding
men to the gospel; then he will be cast into chains,
unable to tempt anybody any more. Today the whole
creation groans and travails in pain; then it shall be
delivered from bondage and corruption. Today Israel
refuses to acknowledge their Messiah; then they will
know and serve their Lord, restored to their land.
Today (and what a pathetic picture it is!) the church
is in humiliation and weakness, the tares and the
wheat grow together. The enemies of the church are
both outside and inside her ranks; she goes through
this wilderness, this time of testing, beset by foes
around, about, beneath, and within. But on that day
she shall reign with Christ! Today the spirit of anti-
christ is manifest everywhere; then he shall be conquered by the power of our God.

In that kingdom which is to come Satan is bound,
the earth is renewed, the church is glorified, the anti-
christ is defeated. The first dramatic event which will
usher in the reign of Jesus is the day when

Some golden daybreak, Jesus will come

and take His people home. For He alone can bind
the devil; He alone can destroy all evil; He alone can
renew the earth. He alone can sift the chaff from the

wheat within the church; in an instant of time He will make His church spotless and pure to glorify Him. Thank God that such heavenly tasks are not left to human achievement.

"Thy kingdom come"—this has been the prayer of the people of God through all the ages. It is the expectation today of our loved ones who are asleep in Jesus and who await their reward until He comes; it is the expectation of the departed believer who is absent from the body and present with the Lord, and who longs to wear a glorified body in which he will be perfect and complete before the throne.

It is the expectation of all creation, says Paul: "For the earnest expectation of the creature waiteth for the manifestation of the sons of God" (Romans 8:19). The whole created universe is under the curse, under the sentence of sin, and waits for the coming of that day when Jesus will complete His elect and take His people home.

It is the expectation of the Lord Jesus Himself, who ". . . when he offered one sacrifice for sin for ever, sat down at the right hand of God; From henceforth expecting till his enemies be made his footstool" (Hebrews 10:12-13). When that prayer is answered, "Thy kingdom come," He will take possession of the kingdom, and ". . . The kingdoms (plural) of this world are become the kingdom (singular) of our Lord, and of His Christ, and He shall reign for ever and ever" (Revelation 11:15).

Therefore, Christian friends, when we pray "Thy kingdom come," let us think of the multitudes of people in the world and in heaven, in the very presence of Christ, with whom we are blending our hearts and voices expressing the burden of our desire, "Lord Jesus, come quickly and set up Thy throne!" What an answer that will be to all the perplexities of the Christian life, all the burdens and conflicts and battles of it! What an answer it will be to all the suffering and tragedy of broken hearts and broken homes! There is no complete solution to such problems until the King comes.

It is not only the kingdom of glory for which we pray, however, but also for the personal kingdom of grace. In Romans 14:17 we read, ". . . the kingdom of God is not meat and drink; but righteousness, and peace, and joy in the Holy Ghost." Now we need to be very clear about one aspect of this message, that the kingdom of glory and the kingdom of grace are very intimately connected the one with the other; they are not two separate things. Unless Jesus Christ reigns as king in my life, and unless I am a born-again member of the kingdom of His grace, I shall never reign with Him in the kingdom of glory. Unless I am a member of the one I can never participate in the other. Unless I have bowed my knee before my Saviour and acknowledged Him as my Lord here, then one day I shall kneel before Him and acknowledge Him as my Judge. I *must* meet this Lord Jesus Christ as King.

I want to emphasize that Christian people cannot afford to play with the false doctrine that you may have a Saviour without having a King. Jesus Christ does not come into your life on the basis of democracy; He comes on the basis of dictatorship or He will not come at all. That is not to say that He is a despot (though indeed that is the correct translation of the Greek word for "Lord"); it is not to say that He comes to rule our lives with an iron rod. But Jesus Christ demands the right of kingship so that in the setting up of His kingdom He may destroy in me the kingdom of the flesh and of sin. The establishment of Jesus on the throne of my life dethrones Satan; I cannot possibly attempt to be a citizen of both kingdoms.

I came over to America on what is called an Immigrant Visa. It is quite impossible for me to remain a citizen of the British Empire and at the same time become a citizen of the United States; neither government will tolerate it. If I am to become a citizen of the United States, I must renounce all loyalty to Queen Elizabeth II. I must completely sever my ties with the one country in order to be a citizen of the other.

Now what is true in the material realm is infinitely more true of the spiritual. I must break my ties with Satan if I would be a member of the kingdom of grace. Have you done that? You can make no terms with your old sovereign; you must be prepared to renounce entirely your loyalty to all the works of darkness if you would become a member of the kingdom of grace.

Therefore, unless Christ reigns in our hearts by His Spirit now, we shall never reign with Him in glory.

The promised outward prosperity and peace and righteousness of His kingdom to come is merely the expression of that inward reign of love to God, of trust in Christ, of dependence upon His Spirit which is the experience of every child of God as he walks with the Lord. This kingdom of grace, therefore, into which you are introduced by an experience of the new birth, of which you become a member when you receive Jesus Christ as your Lord, when you bow your heart before Him and acknowledge His sovereignty, is a kingdom in which He is undisputed king, and you are His servant and His subject.

There is so much loose thinking and so much loose teaching today, even in the name of evangelical Christianity, which does not go far enough in my judgment (and certainly not along the line of Scripture), to make perfectly clear that it is impossible for a man to be in the kingdom of grace unless he is seeking to make Jesus Christ the sovereign Lord of his life. I must therefore press this issue upon you with all my heart, because I am concerned that everyone shall be in the kingdom of glory, and I am desperately concerned that you should be a citizen of the kingdom of grace, redeemed by the blood and acknowledging in your life the dictatorship of the Holy Spirit.

I am not referring to politics, but merely stating a fact when I say that in world affairs as well as in church government, democracy is contrary to the New Testament. The final answer in the world is the dictatorship of Jesus Christ. The final answer in the church is the Lordship of the Holy Spirit, expressed through the utter surrender of every member of the church to the authority of the Third Person of the Trinity. In all our church service and church work our one concern is not what we want, nor what this or that committee wants, but "What is the will of God?" "Where does the Holy Spirit want us to go?" He will unfailingly lead the fellowship which is utterly submitted to His Lordship.

This kingdom of grace, therefore, is the personal reign of Jesus Christ in our hearts. You cannot pray, "Thy kingdom come on earth," unless you are honestly willing to pray, "Thy kingdom come in my heart." If you pray, "Thy kingdom come," you acknowledge that you are outside the kingdom by nature, that you are not automatically in it. "Thy kingdom come" reminds me that I am a sinner, and the consequence of my sin is that I am banished from relationship with God; it reminds me that the world lies in the evil one, and all of it is under the bondage of sin which reigns around us. "Thy kingdom come" reminds me that I am a rebel by nature, that I am anti-God, that the flesh hates His authority. When I pray, "Thy kingdom come," I am praying, "O God, take me, a rebel, one who has hated Thy rule and despised Thy authority, and save me by the blood of Jesus Christ. Come into my heart and make me a citizen and a glad subject of Thy kingdom. Change this rebel heart of mine, and make it come to Thee in utter surrender to Thy feet."

Again, when you pray, "Thy kingdom come," you

acknowledge that you cannot enter into the kingdom of yourself, but it must come to you. Prayer, piety, religion, good works—these are not the way into the kingdom. The kingdom must come, and Jesus must come Himself to inhabit our lives.

Let me point out some of the immense practical implications of all this. I have shown you something of the prophetic aspect of the kingdom, and something of the personal kingdom in which He is Lord. What are the practical outworkings of this in your life and mine?

Here is an important parallel between this kingdom of grace and the kingdom of glory. The world cannot gradually merge into the kingdom or reach it by development and effort—and neither can we! We may gradually become aware of what has happened, but the fact of the matter is that in an instant of time, in answer to your faith in what Jesus did for you on the cross and in answer to your receiving Christ into your heart and life, at that moment you pass from death to life, from darkness to light, from the kingdom of Satan to the kingdom of God—in a flash! There is no such thing as gradually getting into the kingdom!

How many people speak to me about their souls and say, "Well, of course I'm not good enough to be a Christian . . . I'll have to wait . . . I'll have to work hard at it . . . I'll have to improve my moral standards . . . clean up my life." If you offer such excuses, I can only say to you that if you don't come now, you may never have the opportunity to come again. It is an immediate crisis—when a soul passes out of darkness into light.

Furthermore, in the kingdom which is to come on earth, God in Jesus Christ will establish His righteousness and His justice. When the kingdom of grace is set up in my heart by a new birth, at that moment Jesus Christ imparts His righteousness in the person of the Holy Spirit in order that my life might be clean and pure. In the kingdom of glory which is to come, "He makes wars to cease to the ends of the earth," and He brings peace. In the kingdom of grace, when Jesus Christ is Lord, there is an end of that awful battle with myself, and the battle with the will of God, and the fight against that which I know to be right. It is the dawn of peace. Of course I know that another conflict with the devil begins. But when every rebellion and controversy against God is ended in my heart, and when Jesus Christ has come to make wars to cease and to establish peace, at that moment I can go out into conflict with the enemy and win every battle—as long as there is peace in my heart with the Lord.

If that kingdom of grace is established in your heart, you can know it without any shadow of a doubt: you will seek to give yourself to Him and to His service that by every means you know you may win others to Christ. You will seek to hasten the day of His coming when that kingdom of glory will be established. If the kingdom of grace is in your heart, then the burden of that heart will be that the kingdom of glory might come. Is that your burden?

Because the kingdom of grace is established, and Jesus Christ is Lord, you will evidence the fact by concern to live your life according to the principles of that kingdom. There are certain things that a citizen of the British Empire can do in Britain that he cannot do elsewhere; there are certain things that a citizen of the United States can do in this country that are prohibited in other lands. When we come into the kingdom of grace, what do we do? We look for the charter of the kingdom, the principles upon which our lives are to be lived.

Where do we find them? Matthew, chapters five, six, and seven—the Sermon on the Mount, right at the heart of which is the Lord's Prayer. It is in the very setting of the charter of the kingdom that we pray, "Thy kingdom come." If the kingdom of grace is in our hearts today, and Jesus is Lord, then the kingdom of glory will be the burden of our desire and our concern will be to save others while there is time. We will evidence that concern by living our lives according to the principles of the kingdom as revealed by the Lord Jesus. Are we doing that?

Some people say that the Sermon on the Mount is purely law: it is, but it is the law of the Spirit of life in Christ to be fulfilled in every believer. Are you a member of that kingdom? Is He your undisputed Sovereign? If He is, then your prayer will be, "Grant, O God, that Thy kingdom may come on earth. Take my life and use it, make it available to Thee so that through me Thy kingdom may be forwarded and the purposes of God fulfilled." Is your prayer today, "Lord Jesus, teach me to live my life through Thine indwelling power in accordance with the charter of the kingdom"?

Chapter IV

Thy Will Be Done

The "Lord's Prayer" is set right in the center of the charter which God has given to those who are the children of His kingdom. It appears in the very heart of the Sermon on the Mount, the ethic for every Christian life which we are enabled by the indwelling Christ to demonstrate in everyday circumstances.

This prayer, therefore, is our family prayer, in which we pray "Our Father." Then, having come to know God in Jesus Christ, how gladly our hearts say, "Thy will be done"! If we reversed that order, it would simply mean sullen, reluctant submission to a God we do not know. But when we know God as our Father in Jesus Christ, as we are in His family, it should be the greatest delight of every Christian to pray, "Thy will be done."

We shall observe as we study this chapter that our Father in heaven has a name we must hallow. He has a kingdom which we must establish. He has a will that we must obey. For this prayer is not merely prophetic of the future, it is practical in relation to the church and to the child of God today.

"Our Father which art in heaven" governs every relationship of our lives in every detail. "Hallowed be Thy name" weighs our every thought, word, and deed. "Thy kingdom come" sets up in each of our lives the undisputed sway of the Holy Spirit. "Thy will be done"—oh, the joy of submitting, down to the last detail of our experience, to the good and perfect and acceptable will of God!

But the only obedience which is really possible to the Christian comes from a heart which loves. True obedience springs only from love; it is because we love Him that we desire to do His will.

"Thy will be done"—so often we pray it thoughtlessly, without recognizing the depth of truth that lies in it. This prayer anticipates a day when the will of God shall be done on earth as it is in heaven, for obedience to the will of God is the ultimate purpose of God for every one of His children. Why? Because only in submission to the will of God is there peace for the world and peace for the human heart.

I ask you to think for a moment upon this world of ours. It does not take much reflection to realize that the will of God is not being done. Man has chosen his own will; he has a plan for himself quite apart from the will of God. He has chosen to live in rebellion against his Creator and Maker. And when we pray, "Our Father . . . Thy will be done in earth as it is in heaven," we pray that no longer should the human will be contrary to our Father's will, but that the whole earth should move in harmony with the purpose and will of God. Every time we breathe this prayer we touch upon the root of all human suffering and pray for its removal.

But if that is true in the outward look, I ask you also to look within your own heart, to examine your own life. Ask yourself if it is not true that the cause of all unrest, all frustration, all unhappiness, all feeling of inability, and all sense of powerlessness in our human character, even though it be the character of a child of God, is the same self-will. The source of these things lies in the fact that, quite frankly, we have not submitted to the will of God.

I say without hesitation that if every Christian in our churches was submitted to God's will, we would have continuous revival. The whole tragedy in the church is that Christian men and women, born again, redeemed by the blood, indwelt by the Spirit, still raise their big capital "I" and refuse to bend before the Lord. The thing that puts the brake on Holy Spirit revival, that raises the bar against God's mighty blessing and the outpoured floodtide of Holy Spirit power, is Christian men and women who do not submit to the omnipotent will of God.

My friend, how much do we desire revival? How much do we really care that God should break through and pour out His blessing? We talk about it, but how much do we really pray about it? If we pray for revival and plead with God to bless, and yet in our lives refuse to submit to His will, we are hypocrites. Before revival comes, perhaps God will either have to remove some of us or break us.

Both the outward and the inward look reveal that the will of God is not being done. Because it is not being done in the Christian, there is no blessing in the church. And because there is no blessing in the church, the world is unreached, untouched, going to hell, lost for time and eternity. May He have mercy upon us and help us to see this awful sin in the church of Christ today! We say we care about lost souls; we say we are burdened for the need of men who have never heard the gospel; we say we long to see our cities reached for Christ. Yet all the time in our hearts there is a big capital "I" which has never been broken and is standing in the way.

Let me ask you, therefore, in the light of its significance, to realize for a moment the heavenly pattern set out in this petition. "Thy will be done in earth"—then what sweet music follows—"as it is in heaven." If we could only glance into that heavenly realm, if only the Holy Spirit would draw back for a moment the veil, what do you think we would see? First we would see something that already we can see to some extent with our naked eye: the created universe, the sun, moon, and stars, all moving swiftly through space together, not one of them ever out of place, singing in the harmony of a creation that is living in the will of God.

But we would see something else: we would see surrounding the throne of heaven, a blood-washed host of the redeemed who have been removed from this scene of corruption and sin and failure, those who are "absent from the body and present with the Lord." We would see them as they are now "safe in the arms of Jesus." We would see a host of angels who minister the government of the throne of God moving swiftly in worship and in service, whose whole desire is centered in the Man upon the throne. Their interest has always been centered in the Lamb of God: they came to announce His birth; they ministered to Him in the wilderness; they strengthened Him in the garden; they announced His resurrection. And today they gather in countless numbers, bowing before the throne of God and crying, "Worthy is the Lamb that was slain!"

Oh, to have just a glimpse within the veil and to see heaven as it is! To see the will of God being done with not one creature out of harmony! To see obedience in which there is no failure because there is no sin! To see obedience that is rendered perfectly because there is no temptation! And then to pray, "Our Father, Thy will be done in earth as it is in heaven." Christian friends, when we pray that, we pray that from one extremity of God's created universe to the other all will be perfect harmony in doing the will of God.

This world of ours has not been abandoned to the devil. It is yet to be the scene of the greatest triumph of God. This earth, which began with the miracle of creation, which has seen the devastation of Satan, and which has witnessed the miracle of the empty tomb, is once again to see the glory of God and experience the reign of Jesus Christ our Lord. This is the fulfillment for which we pray, "Thy will be done in earth as it is in heaven."

Somebody may say, "That is utterly impossible. It never has been done; it never could be done on this earth." As a matter of fact, it has been done already; the will of God has been perfectly accomplished down here. There came from heaven one day a Man who took upon Him the form of a servant, humbled Himself, and became obedient even unto the death of the cross. Therefore we can say to you that flesh and blood, in the person of the spotless Son of God, has fulfilled completely the will of God.

Pause for a moment to remember the darkness of approaching Calvary, when in Gethsemane He was overshadowed by the consciousness that He was to be "made sin for us, who knew no sin." The weight of the burden that He was about to bear almost crushed Him. It was not physical pain, nor the valley of death at which He trembled, for He knew He would overcome them. It was because God, in whose smile He had lived from all eternity, was about to turn His face from Him. It was because He was about to enter into darkness, and to taste of death and condemnation on behalf of each one of us. It was because the anger and wrath of God toward sin was to break in all its fury upon Him.

In Gethsemane, as He sweated great drops of blood, He cried, "Oh my Father, if it be possible, let this cup pass from me: nevertheless not as I will, but as thou wilt." He picked Himself up from the ground, and an angel appeared and ministered unto Him. He took up the cross and bore it upon His shoulders, and He went up that "green hill outside a city wall." When I read the language of my Bible, I become more and more amazed as I recognize the significance of it: ". . . it pleased the Lord to bruise him . . ." (Isaiah 53:10).

As in Gethsemane He went through all the implications of His coming sacrifice, what do you think hurt Him most? What was the greatest grief He had to bear? It was not the mocking and spitting of the crowd. True indeed, He was to be made sin for us, who knew no sin. He was to go under the judgment of God. That brought Him down in weakness, and He prayed that it might be possible for it to be averted, but He went through with God's will to the last inch and He obeyed it.

Surely the thing that broke His heart, and that made it almost unbearable, was the kiss of a treacherous disciple who had refused God's will and chosen his own. In spite of the taunts and thorns, in spite of all the attacks of Satan, and in spite, most of all, of the kiss of a man who betrayed Him, He said, "Father, forgive them, for they know not what they do." He answered the prayer of a dying thief, and He committed His own dear mother to a disciple

whom He loved. He drank to the dregs the cup the
Father gave Him: "My meat is to do the will of him
that sent me, and to finish his work."

"It is done!" He cried. "Thy will, My Father, be
done in earth as it is in heaven."

When we pray, "Thy will be done," do we understand the cost of it in our lives? Can the will of God
be done today—not merely in the ages to come, but
right here and now? Indeed it can!

At the back of all our failures (God forgive us)
is a desire for *my* way, *not* His way. At the back of
them all is a will that can say "No!" to God in spite
of Calvary. The fact of the matter is, Christian
friends, that though you and I live to be ninety,
going through earth's experiences saved and sanctified, knowing the indwelling Christ, believing the
doctrine, we carry in our breast a nature that is at
enmity to God, and will never be any different. At
any moment the most mature saint may stamp his
heel and lift his head to heaven and say, "No!"

The only possibility of God's will being done in
me is that the Holy Spirit gets hold of my heart, my
mind, my life, and breaks me from all my opposition
so that all His omnipotent power may fulfill it in this
human, earthen vessel. I cannot do it, neither can
you. If, however, I yield to the will of God, I discover that I am utterly conquered and captured by
the God to whom I have yielded! If His will is done,
I discover that it is not by the pressure, nor by the

outward influence of other people, but by an inward Person flooding my heart and life with the love of Jesus Christ. ". . . this is the will of God, even your sanctification . . ." (I Thessalonians 4:3).

We are utterly mistaken if we think that in praying, "Father in heaven, Thy will be done," and in submitting to the will of God we are weak and spineless. That is what the Communist says about the Christian, and that is why he is determined to wipe out Christianity. The Communist insists that at the very heart of the Christian faith there is a principle of surrender, and he believes in "No surrender!" He imagines, therefore, that the Christian is weak and spineless, and useless as a tool for world revolution.

On the contrary, the Christian subjected to the Holy Spirit and utterly submissive to the will of God is the mightiest factor in world revolution to bring about God's kingdom. The Communist with his bombs and his atheism, his corruption and his vice, has no power! The man of God, redeemed and indwelt by the Holy Spirit, the child of God, as meek as a little infant in his relationship with God, is mighty in his relationship to the world, by the power of God.

It is failure on the part of Christians to be submissive to the will of God which makes the church weak and divided. It is failure to face surrender in his own life which makes the minister powerless. I am not talking to you about something I have merely

read in my Bible, but about something I have expe-
rienced, and I suppose you are like me in that. Sometimes a preacher will plead with God that He will
"do what the preacher cannot do." Somehow I think
I never really did much as the outcome of what
somebody preached at me from a pulpit. But I lived
ten years of my Christian life in an utter wilderness.
And I lived subsequent years, preaching to other
people in the early days of my Christian ministry,
knowing perfectly well that deep down in my heart
were things I wasn't prepared to yield to my Lord.
I'm in the school now, thank God, although only in
the kindergarten, so to speak. I have discovered already that the only possibility of peace is absolute
submission to the will of God.

What do I mean by that? Go back a minute to the
pattern, "Thy will be done in earth as it is in
heaven." The will of God is done in heaven constantly, without failure. Am I only intermittent in
my allegiance and obedience—do I fail from time to
time? The will of God is done in heaven universally,
without exception.

Do I make selections from God's commands, pick
and choose as to which ones I should obey? Do I
make exceptions and say, "Yes, Lord I will obey You
here, but I won't obey You there"? Am I one man on
my knees and another man when I am on my feet?
Am I humble in prayer, but proud in my business?
Am I submissive in my church, but an autocrat in
my business life? Am I as sweet as honey in the fel-

lowship of God's house, but like a devil inspired with my wife and children? Do I make exceptions, or do I obey God in every detail?

Are there some things here that are going right home to you? Have you been selective as to what is the will of God? Are there issues in your life on which you are not utterly surrendered, points of resistance to the Holy Spirit which He has never broken through, and the will of God is not being done, and you are not being used?

In heaven the will of God is done joyfully, without weariness. Do I tire of doing God's will? Sometimes this preacher gets mighty near it, for the will of God is not the easiest thing to do; it goes too deep and it hurts too much. In heaven the will of God is done humbly, without glory to anyone but Jesus. If I do the will of God, do I make it known that in this issue and that one I have done God's will, and I am progressing?

"Thy will be done in me, O Lord, as it is in heaven"—constantly, universally (in every part of my life), instantly (without hesitation), obediently, joyfully, humbly.

Do you think I am expecting a standard and adding a burden which is impossible? "Not every one that saith unto me, Lord, Lord, shall enter into the kingdom of heaven"; said Jesus, "but he that doeth the will of my Father which is in heaven" (Matthew 7:21). I set no higher a standard than that!

But listen to the precious promise that He adds:

". . . whosoever shall do the will of God, the same is my brother, my sister, and my mother."

". . . he that doeth the will of God abideth for ever."

Chapter V

Our Daily Bread

This prayer has moved from worship—"Our Father which art in heaven," through adoration—"hallowed be Thy name," through missionary zeal, which is always the outcome of worship and adoration of God—"Thy kingdom come," to a place where we have abandoned all interest in ourselves in a supreme desire for the will of God to "be done in earth as it is in heaven."

Having risen to those heights, it seems something of an anticlimax to hear, "Give us this day our daily bread." The first part of the prayer has been so self-less, and this seems so selfish; the first has been so comprehensive, and this seems so narrow. What a collapse—what a failure, surely—suddenly to cease from worship and to ask God for food for our body!

To be occupied one moment with a desire for the will of God, to lose everything in that great longing and concern for His glory, then suddenly to ask for our daily food! How feeble!

But is it? Prayer is not only adoration; it is asking.

"If ye then, being evil," said the Lord Jesus, "know how to give good gifts unto your children, how much more shall your Father which is in heaven give good things to them that ask him?" (Matthew 7:11). ". . . ye have not," said James, "because ye ask not" (James 4:2). Prayer is worship, but it is also specific, definite asking.

You will notice how the first part of this prayer has gone from the inner shrine of worship to the outward sphere of service. It began in heaven, and then it sought to bring heaven down to earth, that heaven and earth might move in harmony and in unison: "Thy will be done in earth as it is in heaven." But this second part of the prayer reverses the direction. It begins with outward want, and then it moves in through sin, through conflict, through temptation, and finally it ends with praise. It speaks about a present need, our bread for today. It speaks about a past failure, "Forgive us our debts." It anticipates future perils on the journey, "Lead us not into temptation." Somehow this family prayer takes within its scope every experience of human life.

The first part of the prayer began with a contemplation of the greatness of our Father in heaven, but the second part starts with a simple cry to God for bread, and it climbs up through our need and through our unforgiving spirit, through our weakness in temptation, and finally it passes through all our sorrows and all our troubles and takes us right home to God. The doxology at the end comes circling around to meet the invocation of "Our Father" at the beginning. This prayer, which has winged its way through all experiences of sorrow and trouble and sadness of life returns, like the dove to Noah's Ark, and finds its home in God.

Oh, that you and I might learn to pray like that!

We come now to the central petition of this prayer, "Give us this day our daily bread." How glibly we pray that, and how readily we pray it! When I think about it, however, I find there is so much behind it all that I scarcely know where to begin.

First of all, this prayer suggests our absolute dependence upon God for everything. In front of us there is conflict, there is temptation, there is need—all the battle of life confronts us. We come to Him with this petition, and we say, "Lord, give us today our daily bread." In praying that we are reminding our hearts, and we are reminding our God, that we dare not face the battle of life without Him, that we are dependent upon Him for every detail. Instead of this plea for daily bread being out of place, the very fact that it finds a central place in the family prayer is the most significant thing about it. The Father whom we have worshiped, the kingdom for which we have prayed, the will for which we have longed —we depend upon Him for them all. The conflict we are about to face, the temptation we have to go through, the battles of life that confront us—we dare not go ahead without reminding ourselves that God is our Father, without confessing our weaknesses, without acknowledging that apart from His strength we must fail.

This prayer relates our Father in heaven to every detail of our lives and it teaches us that there is nothing in life too small to bring to God. Once we begin to think that things are too insignificant to trouble God with, and that our need is too small to bother Him, we begin to sow the seed of unbelief, which means that we will not merely omit taking little things, but one day we will fail to take the big things to God. Just as the tallest skyscraper that has ever been built, from the top of which can be seen the whole city and surrounding country, has to have its foundation upon common earth, so this prayer reminds us that the most spiritually minded Christian must keep his feet on the ground and realize that he is dependent upon his God for the supply of his every need.

"Our Father, give us this day our daily bread."

This prayer also expresses our conviction and belief that God is able to answer our prayer and to meet our needs. It is not that we are praying to take something from God which He is unwilling to give, or that we are trying to overcome His reluctance, seeking to bend His will to ours; it is rather that we are taking hold of God's willingness to give. We have claimed our relationship and have reminded Him that He is our Father through faith in Jesus Christ.

We have prayed for His kingdom, and for His will; we have told Him that we desire only that His will be done in our lives and in the world. Now we declare that He is able to give, and we are right! For it is our God's chief and greatest delight to give to His children.

When there was no other way of deliverance, when all the world was in darkness, helpless to save itself, ". . . God so loved the world, that he gave his only begotten Son. . . ." He has proved His love; He has proved His power; and He is longing to meet our need. When God gives, He gives lavishly and unstintingly: "He that spared not his own Son, but delivered him up for us all, how shall he not with him also freely give us all things?" (Romans 8:32).

Someone has said that the greatest of saints are the greatest receivers: those who know their own helplessness, those who refuse to carry one burden or anxiety themselves, those who cast all the responsibility for their welfare upon their God.

> When we have exhausted our store of endurance,
> When our strength has failed 'ere the day is half done,
> When we reach the end of our hoarded resources,
> The Father's full giving has only begun.
> His love has no limits; His grace has no measure,
> His power no boundary known unto men;
> For out of His infinite riches in Jesus
> He giveth and giveth and giveth again.

Oh, that Christian men and women, fellows and girls, would cease to tap their own feeble resources and realize that our Father in heaven loves to give! He is able to meet our every need. The growth of Christian character is always marked by going more and more often as a pauper to God in the name of the living, all-prevailing Saviour, and taking to our Father in heaven the smallest detail of life, believing that God loves to give.

This prayer also expresses our belief that He will supply the greatest necessities of life. Although the primary meaning of this petition is request for material food, when we pray for our daily bread, we realize that every piece of bread we eat means that a corn of wheat has fallen into the ground and died, that the ultimate source of everything is from God. That leads us to remember the One who is the Bread of Life sent down from heaven that a man may eat thereof and not die. The Lord Jesus said, "... Man shall not live by bread alone, but by every word that proceedeth out of the mouth of God" (Matthew 4:4), and except we eat this bread we have no life in us.

The deepest necessity of life is not simply for the needs of the body, but for Jesus Christ as the Saviour of the soul. When we pray, "Give us this day our daily bread," in effect we pray, "Lord, give me this day Jesus—in all His strength to match my weakness, in all His patience to meet my haste and feverishness, in all His purity to meet my sin. Lord, give me this day Jesus, my share of Him who is on the throne, a risen, glorified Master and Lord."

I remind you, also, that this prayer does not say, "Give *me*," it says, "Give *us* this day our daily bread." When we come together around the Lord's table in the local fellowship of a church, we are reminded that all the family of God, missionaries and converts in all parts of the world, all Christians behind the Iron and Bamboo curtains, every child of God everywhere, gather within the scope of this prayer, "Give *us* this day our daily bread." The church of Christ on earth today, often baffled and perplexed, torn and suffering, tempted and tried, battling against the world, the flesh, and the devil, looks up to a heavenly Father and says, "Give us, today, Jesus!"

How wonderful it is to know that no one ever comes to the Father's table like that and goes away hungry, for even ". . . the dogs eat of the crumbs that fall from . . . (the) table." None of us can come to worship, lifting up our hearts to Him and saying, "O Father, give me this day Jesus in all His riches and power, beauty and glory, grace and love, meekness and patience. Give me Jesus!"—none of us can utter that prayer and go unanswered. This petition expresses the conviction that He will supply today the greatest necessity of life, even Christ Himself to our hearts.

But it expresses something else, also—our trust in God's method of giving: "Give us *this day* our daily bread."

> Strength for each trial and each task:
> What more, my Saviour, should I ask?

Yesterday's strength is absolutely useless for today. May God save us, as Christian people, from relying on an experience of yesterday! Many a man lives his Christian life on the experience of years ago. It is literally years since he has felt a fresh touch of the grace of God upon his soul and upon his life. Often his life is as dry as dust; his bread is stale and the world knows it! Such a man is looking back upon the past of his life, and there he is drawing upon moldy bread, while this prayer talks of "daily bread."

How many have a testimony, but it is out of date? How many have the bread of life, but it has gone stale and sour? How many of us, when we meet the world, make no impression upon the unbeliever because we are not being fed day by day from the Word of God? Far too many Christian people regard their minister as a kind of spiritual milk bottle, who feeds them on Sunday mornings to keep them going for seven days until they meet again! But when we pray this prayer we say, "Our Father, give me (each day of the week—give me today) Jesus, my daily Bread," and we find that God is not the God of yesterday, but the God of today. This means that through the avenues of each day's life I can expect to meet God again, that today I can have new supplies from Him, that I can meet with Jesus in my home, in the street, anywhere, and may receive from my Lord today my daily bread.

This prayer does not say anything about tomorrow; future supplies are not our concern. It is daily bread, fresh from the oven, and it is enough for today. God never gives a man stores of grace or a reservoir from which he can draw. You may have an automobile that is capable of taking seventeen gallons of gas. That will keep you going for 200 or 250 miles, then you fill up again. You may not have an automobile, and instead you use the street car, which has no gas tank in it, nor storage for electricity. All it does is to keep its arm in contact with the source of power. It does not see where the power is coming from, nor does it worry about how it is going to get to the end of the line, for all the time its arm is in moment-by-moment contact with the source of power.

Your spiritual life is not fed upon the storage plan. It is maintained on the contact plan. Moment by moment your life needs to be in contact with the Lord:

> Moment by moment I'm kept in His love,
> Moment by moment I've life from above.

That is Christian experience, being in constant contact with the source of power. The Christian who enjoys that experience does not worry about tomorrow. He is living to enjoy the grace of God today, and he expects the same God to meet with him tomorrow.

It was D. L. Moody who said once that he did not desire grace to die for Christ, all he wanted was grace to preach for Him right now. John Wesley was asked by one of his friends, "Supposing, Mr. Wesley, you knew that this was to be your last night on earth, how would you spend it?"

"Well, at four o'clock I would have some tea," he replied "and at six o'clock I would visit Mrs. Brown in the hospital. Then at seven-thirty I would conduct mid-week service at this chapel. At nine-ten I would have my supper; at ten o'clock I would go to bed, and in the morning I would wake up in glory!"

That is moment-by-moment, day-by-day trust in the living Lord Jesus. Are you living your life like that?

What a difference it makes to know that God will never lead us into any place where He will not come with us. He knows the line of our march; He knows the route that He wants us to take, and He will map it out day by day. He will issue the instructions every morning, and therefore each day will have its sunshine, each cloud will have its rainbow, and if we are led into dry and thirsty land, He will open fountains in the desert—He will cause it to blossom like the rose. If we are led out of places of revival into places of death, where there is no blessing, God is there, the same God who has guaranteed to supply our every need according to His riches in glory by Christ Jesus. That puts a thrill into Christian experience, and takes all the dullness and monotony out of it!

Why do we fear tomorrow? Why do we doubt? If we trust today for God's grace to match our need, we can leave tomorrow to Him, for ". . . sufficient unto the day is the evil thereof."

That is the principle of God's giving. He is not going to give you grace to do something tremendous tomorrow. He is going to give you grace to be extraordinary in the ordinary circumstances of today. He is not concerned about you doing anything wonderful; He is concerned about you being wonderful in everyday life. Day by day you will receive your daily bread.

This petition also expresses our recognition that every detail of life must be consecrated to the Lord. You cannot pray this prayer and then seek to get your daily bread by unworthy means. You cannot say, "Lord, bless my sharp practices in business. Bless my laziness. Bless my indolence. Bless my cheating." I suggest you make this a test: "Give me this day my daily bread." If you dare not pray that over what you call earning your living, you should ask yourself whether in fact you are earning your death.

If I pray, "Give me this day my daily bread," that means I am depending upon God for my daily need, and that my business will produce that need, no more and no less. It means to say that sharp practice, quick profit, shady dealing, are cut out, for I cannot ask God to bless these things, and at the same time pray this prayer. It recognizes that every detail of life has to be consecrated to the Lord.

Lastly, this prayer expresses our readiness to accept the kind of bread that God supplies. "Give us this day our daily bread," is not really a very good translation—it conveys the sense of somewhat weak repetition. I think a more accurate translation would be this: "Give us this day bread suited to our need." It may be the bread of tears; it may be the bread of adversity; it may be the bread of sorrow. But it always comes from a loving heavenly Father who knows what kind of bread is most suited to the need of His child. Sometimes when we pray this prayer, we are merely asking God to supply our material want, to meet our spiritual need, to give us each day His grace and His power, but sometimes God sends the bread of adversity.

Sometimes we complain against God's food, as the children of Israel complained about the manna in the wilderness—they didn't like it. It was dull and uninteresting. Some of the greatest lessons and some of the most wonderful experiences of Christian living can be learned only if I learn them in this school of obedience and faith, and if I take the kind of food that God knows is suited to my daily requirements.

He knows what is needed to make me like the Lord Jesus, for that is His purpose for all of us. He knows what is needed to channel me into a means of blessing. He knows what is needed to make you and me vessels unto honor, sanctified and meet for the Master's use. He knows what is needed to give us strength in temptation, to give us victory over sin, to give us power to go through life's experiences.

He knows what is needed to make us usable and mighty in His hand anywhere He may send us.

To give us the greatest blessings and to make our most effective service possible, sometimes He pours into the life of His child, almost to the point of breaking it, the bread of adversity, the bread of sorrow, and the bread of affliction. When the child of God learns to digest that heavenly food and to accept it with gladness and singleness of heart, he is on the way to being a man of God.

There is no more awful statement in the Word of God concerning His dealings with Israel than when it is recorded, ". . . he gave them their request; but sent leanness into their soul" (Psalm 106:15). They kicked aganst God's food, His discipline, His chastisement. They wanted something else—a way of less discipline and testing, an easier path. They wanted something to set them free from His law and His authority, and God gave them what they wanted. But He sent poverty into their souls!

God save us from praying a prayer like that! May we never ask Him to stay His hand of discipline or remove His hand of chastisement or take away His hand of adversity if it is through these things He is molding and fashioning us, making us as clay in the hand of the Potter.

"Give me today, Lord Jesus Christ, bread suited for my soul."

This makes my heart echo the prayer of Agur which seems to me the great commentary upon this petition: "Two things have I required of thee; deny me them not before I die; Remove far from me vanity and lies: give me neither poverty nor riches; feed me with food convenient for me" (Proverbs 30:7, 8).

Chapter VI

Forgive Us Our Debts

Up to this point in the family prayer we have been living in the atmosphere of praise and worship. The intimacy of our relationship with our heavenly Father, based upon our receiving Jesus Christ as our Saviour, has led to the natural and inevitable desire that His name should be hallowed, His will be done, His kingdom established. We have rejoiced because of our union with our Father in heaven, and we have expressed that joy by our concern for His glory.

Even the petition which we just considered in the last chapter, the prayer for our daily bread, is prayed in an attitude of confident, expectant hope. With upturned face, in the assurance that He never fails those who put their trust in Him, we have asked for food convenient for us, for bread suited to our need, for daily supplies of His grace to meet our weakness.

But now the tempo of the prayer changes: the clouds seem to gather. Our hearts are filled with sorrow as we turn to examine the past with its awful consciousness of failure, and we say, "Forgive us our debts."

Soon we are to face the perils of the future journey. Soon we are to beg our heavenly Father not to lead us into temptation, but if it is His will to do so, then in the course of temptation to deliver us from evil. But how dare we ask Him to do this? What right have we to expect Him to give daily grace to meet our daily need unless we are sure He has forgiven our debts? Here we echo the words of David in the awful hour of his humiliation, "Wash me thoroughly from mine iniquity, and cleanse me from my sin. . . . Create in me a clean heart, O God; and renew a right spirit within me. . . . a broken and a contrite heart, O God, thou wilt not despise" (Psalm 51:2, 10, 17).

There are three different aspects of this petition. It implies, first of all, the consciousness of sin. Please remember that this is the family prayer; we are talking to our Father in heaven. The only comment upon this prayer which our Lord made was on this one particular petition. You remember He said, "For if ye forgive men their trespasses, your heavenly Father will also forgive you" (Matthew 6:14). We are moving here in the intimacy of the family circle. This is not God speaking to a rebel, but to His child. We are not praying to an unknown God but to our Father, who sent His Son to be our Saviour, and by His blood we have been redeemed. The sin about which we are now concerned is the sin against *our* Father. It is disobedience in your life and mine that commands our thought and attention, and wakes us to a desperate need for forgiveness. "Forgive us *our* debts."

In writing to the church at Ephesus, Paul said, ". . . grieve not the Holy Spirit of God, whereby ye are sealed unto the day of redemption" (Ephesians 4:20). You can grieve only someone who loves you; you cannot grieve a stranger—you may anger or annoy him, but you cannot grieve him. When the child of God sins, he wounds the heart of God and grieves Him. This is sin on the deepest level. Surely we all need to pray thus before Him in a spirit of utter humiliation, with our faces cast down and with our hearts broken, "Father, forgive us *our* debts."

How many of us are conscious of sin at all? We are so thankful that there is now no condemnation to them that are in Christ, and that we are clothed about in the righteousness of the Lord Jesus. But are we completely unaware of sin in our hearts? Certainly we are very conscious of it in the hearts of other people. We are thankful indeed for our position in Christ, but we are thoughtless, too often, of our experience. We can rejoice that we are no longer under the judgment of God. But are we utterly careless of the fact that, though we may be free from God's judgment, constant sin in our lives may be depriving us of His fellowship?

A man who has never tasted God's redeeming grace can, on a certain level, be happy. But a Christian who has been born again, who never seeks the forgiveness of his Father in heaven, who is out of touch with the Lord, is utterly miserable. An overemphasis on our position as believers in Christ without constant regard to our state can result in building up hardness of heart and unresponsiveness of spirit which make us destitute of all evidences of the grace of God.

The prayer for daily bread, you observe, is followed by the prayer for daily forgiveness. Many of us, conscious of our need of daily strength, are utterly unconscious of our need for daily forgiveness. How we excuse our faults by saying, "After all, nobody is perfect!" We are prone to excuse our tempers and our temperaments, our pride and our selfishness, our attitudes and our reactions too lightly by saying, "Oh, Jesus died for our sins, and it is all covered by the blood." But the blood of Jesus Christ was not shed on the cross to enable the child of God to continue in his sin. "God forbid!" I echo the Apostle Paul, ". . . How shall we, that are dead to sin, live any longer therein?" (Romans 6:2). Until that sin—that particular, specific, detailed sin—is taken in all its hideousness to the Lord and confessed and forsaken, our fellowship with our Father is broken.

Are you living out of touch with the Lord? Is there no real sense of His grace and love in your heart? Have you become spiritually hardened, though perhaps doctrinally correct? Why? Although the sin of the child of God can never break relationship with God, which is eternal, it can break fellowship with God, which is temporary. Every time the Christian slips into sin—of thought, of word, of action, of attitude, of mind, of spirit—at that moment he is cut off from fellowship until he goes back to the Lord, who redeemed him and acknowledges his sin, claiming the cleansing of the blood.

". . . if we walk in the light (if we are out in the open about everything with God), as he (the Lord Jesus) is in the light, we have fellowship one with another, and the blood of Jesus Christ his Son, cleanseth us from all sin" (I John 1:7). Failure to realize that principle and to acknowledge our daily sin breaks all possibility of fellowship with Him, and leads to coldness of heart, hardness of spirit, unresponsiveness to the gospel, until we discover our Christian experience seems merely a lifeless shell of doctrine, unfilled with the living fruit of grace.

Is that the portion of some Christians simply because they have never learned the principle that it is utterly necessary to live in the light with the Lord day by day and moment by moment? Many have been led to the false presumption that because they have been forgiven their guilt there is no need to ask further forgiveness, or to confess sin to Him. We are complete in Christ; we stand perfect before God in the Person of our Substitute—that is glorious judicial truth concerning the past. But it does not deal with the vital question of the Christian's fellowship with his Lord today. I am persuaded that the ineffectivness of our testimony—the coldness of our hearts as Christians, our unresponsiveness to the gospel, and the way we are completely bereft of any evidence of God's grace in our lives—is because we do not humble ourselves each day and go to our Lord, pleading with Him for our forgiveness.

The sin of the child of God, which breaks fellowship with Him immediately, ought to break our hearts. It certainly breaks the heart of God.

In referring to sin in the Christian life, I do not refer to some gross moral breakdown, or to some awful transgression of God's law. I am referring to something far more subtle and serious than that. What is sin? The Lord Jesus taught us to pray, "Forgive us our debts." In other words, sin is debt; it is something I owe to my Father in heaven which I have not paid. Do I owe Him anything? What is it I owe? Do I not take of the cup of salvation and thank God for the grace that is so full and free? Yes, indeed! But at the same time, grace is the greatest process of discipline that a Christian can know. The child of God, no longer under the judgment of the law of God, is nevertheless placed in a position where he is obligated to fulfill the law of God by the energy of the Holy Spirit within him, revealed by the grace of God in his heart. Let it never be said that a Christian is exempt from responsibility because he is no longer under law but under grace.

What is my debt to my Father in heaven? "What? know ye not that your body is a temple of the Holy Ghost, . . . and you are not your own? For ye are bought with a price . . ." (I Corinthians 6:19–20). In other words, I owe my heavenly Father my body: my tongue, my hands, my feet: everything! Some Christians have never learned to give Him their tongue, for some do the devil's business in the church of God by gossip with tongues that have never been surrendered to the Lord. How often the tongue that is owed to God has been used in the slander of your brother's and sister's character or reputation! My brother, you are in debt today! You owe Him your body, and it may be that such debt is piling up on a very serious level in your life.

Furthermore, notice this language in Romans 8: ". . . we are debtors, not to the flesh, to live after the flesh. For if ye live after the flesh, ye shall die: but if ye through the Spirit do mortify the deeds of the body, ye shall live" (Romans 8:12–13). In other words, I owe the Lord Jesus Christ my life, that I may live it not according to the dictates of self, but according to the will of His Spirit: "For as many as are led by the Spirit of God, they are the sons of God" (Romans 8:14).

You are in debt to the Lord today if you have failed to live after the Spirit, but have lived after the flesh.

Again, I remind you that Paul said, "I am debtor both to the Greeks, and to the Barbarians . . ." (Romans 1:14). Debtor to preach the gospel, and to proclaim a living Lord Jesus! Every one of us is in debt, there. We owe our heavenly Father our tongue, our hands, our feet, our body. We owe Him our life that it might be lived in the Spirit of God. We owe Him our testimony day by day that others may see Christ in us. Have we ever really searched our hearts about this thing and discovered how deeply and gravely in debt we are?

I believe the language of that great prayer of confession used in the Anglican Church (I am afraid often merely as a formality) is, nevertheless, the language that ought to be on our hearts as we pray and confess that "we have erred and strayed from Thy ways like lost sheep; we have followed too much the devices and desires of our own hearts; we have offended against Thy holy law; we have done the things we ought not to have done; we have left undone those things that we ought to have done, and there is no health in us. O God, have mercy upon us, miserable offenders!"

Perhaps, as we are so aware of sin in the life of the unbeliever, and sometimes so aware of breakdown and failure in the life of our brothers and sisters in Christ, the greatest need of all is that the Holy Spirit of God might speak to our hearts and convince us of the sin in our own soul: "Forgive us *our* debts"! It may be that for the first time some of you are being made conscious that you are in debt to the Lord.

I want you to notice here, also, that after the confession of sin comes the cry for forgiveness: "Forgive us our debts." You will notice that this little phrase is linked with the petition for daily bread by the word "and": "*And* forgive us our debts as we forgive our debtors." The suggestion is that just as we need to go to Him for daily grace for daily need, so we need to go to Him for daily mercy for daily sin.

Someone may say, "But where is the victory in a life like that? What about the ability of the Lord Jesus to deliver from the love of sinning? Is that not a hopeless contradiction?" I must acknowledge that I used to think like that, but I have come to see so clearly from the New Testament that the greatest victory in the life of the child of God is that a man should have a truly humble and contrite heart.

The Christian who always lives at the cross in penitence is the Christian who always lives in fellowship with his Lord in power. Calvary is not a place I visit to get security from hell; it is not a place where I simply go to get my guilt put away and be made right with God; but it is a place where I live every moment of my life. There is no blessing that God can give any of His children who think that they can ever get one inch higher than Jesus' feet. There is no release of Holy Spirit power to the self-life of the child of God. There is no deliverance in His grace and strength until the Christian has learned to go to the cross and stay there every day of his life.

Of course His grace is sufficient, and He gives victory, but we live in a body whose redemption is still future, and all its appetites are with us yet. We are not yet saved from the very presence of sin. "Part of the ministry of the grace of God," as Dr. J. C. Macaulay so beautifully expresses it in his book, *After This Manner,* "is to teach us that 'denying ungodliness and worldly lusts, we should live soberly, righteously and godly in this present world.' Grace is a teacher, and that word means 'chastener.' In other words, it is discipline." One of the greatest sanctifying ministries of the grace of God is to teach us to hate our sins which we used to love, to compare our lives with the pattern set before us in Christ, to confess our sin to Him, and to enjoy His forgiveness.

It is an amazing paradox, but I know it to be true from the lives of the saints of God and from the teaching of the Book, that the heart which eagerly longs for holiness and victory is the heart that is constantly deploring its own corruption. The life that is living in victory is the life that is utterly broken at Calvary, and absolutely dependent upon His indwelling power for everything. Victory in the Christian life is not in you or me—it is in Jesus!

Oh, that we might learn to cry for forgiveness daily in the recognition that as we walk in the light as He is in the light we have fellowship with Him and His blood cleanses from all sin. I wonder how many of us have built up through the years of Christian experience an attitude of hardness to this teaching, a resistance to the Spirit of God, who would point out years of sin in your life which has never been confessed.

But let me speak to you also about the condition of

enjoyment of God's fellowship. "Forgive us our debts, as we forgive our debtors." This little phrase has caused this prayer to be banished from use in some evangelical circles. Some feel this prayer teaches that forgiveness is obtained by merit rather than by the blood of Christ. Let me repeat: this is the *family* prayer we are considering, and it does not deal with the sins of unbelievers. It does not deal with our standing before God, which can *never* be affected; it concerns the sins of the children of God which bar us from His intimate fellowship.

Within the family circle, within the church, and within the family of God, a high standard of performance is expected from those of us who have tasted God's forgiving mercy. Have you understood that the cross of Jesus Christ proclaims something more than atonement—it proclaims example. Not either atonement *or* example, but both atonement *and* example. And the Lord Jesus who cried on Calvary, "Father, forgive them, for they know not what they do!" expects to hear that prayer echoed in the heart of every one of His blood-bought children.

Our Lord makes an explicit comment on this phrase "as we forgive our debtors," in Matthew 6:14–15, ". . . if ye forgive not men their trespasses, neither will your Father forgive your trespasses." Christian friends, we dare not shrink from this, even though it touches pretty deep in our lives. A condition of restored fellowship with Christ within the family of God is a forgiving spirit.

"How often," said Peter, "shall my brother sin and I forgive him? Seven times?" ("Pretty generous," thought Peter, "After all, if a fellow is going to sin against me seven times running, there is not much hope for him—might as well give him up!") How many times am I willing to forgive the man who hurts and wounds me and sins against me?

Jesus looked him in the face and said, "Peter, unto seventy times seven!" In other words, there is no limit! "There is no limit to My love for you, Peter, or to the length to which I am willing to go in redeeming you, so that there must be no limit to your love toward the man who hates you."

The man who would seek God's forgiveness for sins committed as a Christian within the family will seek it in vain unless he shows forgiveness to other people. In other words, the evidence that God has forgiven you is that you forgive other people. That you have tasted of God's redeeming love is borne out by the fact that gladly and lovingly you forgive all others.

Consider for a moment the separations which develop, the resentments which arise out of injuries and slights, real or imagined, thoughtlessly committed years ago. The original cause often is so stupidly small compared with its awful outcome in broken friendships and broken homes. How often our relationships with other people are governed entirely by their criticism of us, and if that is true, what an appalling revelation it is of how much we love ourselves, and how important we think we are!

"Can I never get my own back, not even once?"
No, my friend, not even once! Why? Because your
experience of God's forgiving mercy to you when He
welcomed you as a sinner for Jesus' sake will make it
impossible for you ever to demand your rights from
other people. Because as a child of God, fellowship
with Christ should matter to you more than anything,
and He will always deny fellowship with Himself
until you forgive other people. You come to church,
you even come to prayer meetings, carrying the resentment of years, carrying the bitterness of a lifetime, and when you ask God for blessing, you wonder why your prayers are not answered, your Bible
is dead, and your devotional life has gone to pieces.

Here is the greatest victory in the Christian life!
". . . when he was reviled, reviled not again, . . .
but committed himself to him that judgeth righteously" (I Peter 2:23). When the proud, stiff-necked
"I" in me has remembered His mercy to me, it cries,
"Father, nothing matters to me but fellowship with
Thee! I cannot go on if I am denied an open heaven
and intimate communion with God. I cannot preach
the gospel or live for Christ if heaven is shut because
of something sinful in my life. I must know that an
ungrieved Holy Spirit is resident in my heart." If I
grieve Him and confess it to Him, I am so glad He
forgives!

When I remember God's mercy at the cross and
every trace of resentment vanishes, then I can go to
the brother who has wronged me or spoken unkindly
and untruthfully about me and tell him that I love

him for Jesus' sake. That is victory! When that happens, the haughtiness in my life becomes love; the bitterness becomes grace; the pride becomes lowliness. Instead of self there will be Jesus, and the angels of heaven rejoice over a soul that demonstrates its salvation with a loving, tender heart, like Christ's, toward others.

Is it hard for someone to forgive? Hard for a resentment to be killed and for it all to be forgotten? Hard for a bitterness against your sister or brother, husband, wife, or child, to die? But if you love the Lord Jesus, you will refuse to let the thing go on one more minute. Though you know that you are right, you will go to your brother lovingly and say, "How I thank God for you, and I thank God for the means of grace which has humbled me through your attitude toward me." No, that is not weakness, but meekness.

Yes, it is always unpleasant to be a doormat, to have people wipe their feet on you, but I remind you of these verses which are constantly in my mind:

> May the mind of Christ my Saviour
> Live in me from day to day,
> By His love and power controlling
>   All I do and say.
>
> May the love of Jesus fill me
> As the waters fill the sea;
> Him exalting, self abasing,
>   This is victory.

May His beauty rest upon me
As I seek the lost to win,
And may they forget the channel,
     Seeing only Him.

Chapter VII

Lead Us Not Into Temptation

This is a prayer of constant movement. The first section of it, which has to do with God, moves from the inner shrine of worship, "Our Father, which art in heaven," to the outer sphere of service, "Thy will be done in earth as it is in heaven." The second part, which has to do with ourselves, moves from the outer place of material necessity, "Give us this day our daily bread," right down to the inner realm of spiritual conflict, "Lead us not into temptation, but deliver us from evil."

But this prayer as a whole moves in still another direction. It moves from the throne of God to the very depths of human experience, and then back again in victory and in praise to the throne. "Our Father which art in heaven"—and what higher calling can there be for any of us than to know that we are the sons of God, redeemed by the blood of Christ. Then we find ourselves worshiping in reverence, on our knees in humility before God—"Hallowed be thy name." "Thy kingdom come"—here we acknowledge that we are subjects of the King, ready to strive for the advancement of His kingdom. "Thy will be done"—and we take our place as slaves, waiting to obey His orders in our lives. "Give us this day our daily bread" —we become beggars and paupers.

As we repeat this prayer, we go down, down the ladder. But even as we cry to our God, dependent on Him for every necessity, we are not at the bottom. We still have to see ourselves as sinners: "Forgive us our debts, as we forgive our debtors"—and we discover with deep conviction our deep need. "Lead us not into temptation"—here we touch the very depths, for not only are we sinners, but we are desperately afraid that we should be even more sinful.

Having come down from the heights to the depths, however, we begin to rise again. "Deliver us from evil"—and here we become warriors in the spiritual battle against the world, the flesh, and the devil. "Deliver us from evil, for Thine is the kingdom, the power, and the glory forever"—here we are victors in the fight; we are discovering the secret of drawing on the King's resources. And at the end of it all: "Amen and amen"—the fight is ended, the battle finished, the sword laid aside, as we ascend into the eternal presence of our God.

That is the Lord's prayer. We begin at our Father's

throne, and we go down to the depths of human weakness, but we rise again to the throne of God to meet our Lord face to face.

It is also, of course, a picture of our growth in Christian experience. In the early days of Christian life we cry, "Our Father," as we enter into that new relationship through faith in Jesus Christ our Lord, being born again by His Spirit. We can call God "Our Father."

Then we begin to worship Him; we seek to be used by Him and become concerned about doing His will. We quickly discover how dependent we are upon Him in every detail of our lives, and we begin really to understand what sin is. Many people are saved without a very deep conviction of sin, but no one is ever a pupil in the school of holiness without discovering how sinful he is. The child of God who began so happily to say, "Our Father," finds himself humbled and humiliated as he goes on in Christian experience. For the flesh is still within him. The Spirit wars against the flesh, and the flesh against the Spirit, and the child of God discovers he has entered into a tremendous conflict. He must give himself up in utter surrender to God, entering into the warfare with complete dependence on the grace of God if he is to triumph, if he would taste of victory. And then one day he will rejoice to see the Saviour in whose power he has won through. That is the Christian life, my friend, and you and I are all in it together.

But let us seek to analyze this realm of inner conflict: "Lead us not into temptation." I do not understand the Christian who says he is unaware of any conflict of soul: this is a realm which should be familiar to every one of us. We have prayed, "Forgive us our debts"—that concerns the past. But now we pray, "Lead us not into temptation," and that concerns the future. Of course, they are very closely related, for the experience of God's forgiving mercy to the Christian has always a threefold effect on his life.

First, it makes him realize his own weakness. The fact that we have sinned takes away all confidence in our own strength. Then forgiveness also makes the child of God long to be holy. No Christian who claims to be washed in the blood of the Lamb can be anything but a hypocrite unless the outcome of such an experience is an intense desire in his heart for holiness. Many Christian people are afraid of that word "holiness." They are afraid of extremes; they are afraid of fanaticism. I would to God that we were more afraid of sin! When a man looks up into the forgiving face of God, he hungers and thirsts after a pure and a godly life. He begins to hate the things that he used to love, to loathe the things to which once he was wedded. He seeks to discover the secret of walking with God in victory.

Again, God's forgiving mercy to us makes us realize how powerful sin is, that even the deep experience of forgiveness has not rooted out of our lives the tendency to sin. In Dr. J. C. Macaulay's book on the Lord's prayer, *After This Manner*, there is this choice phrase: "The loathing which we have of sin in the holy moment of pardon strangely weakens when we find ourselves in the old atmosphere, with the old temptation wearing its most alluring garb. Our high resolve does not come to our rescue fast enough when temptation hits us like a thunderbolt."

How many times we claim God's forgiveness for the same sin! We stamp our foot in resolve and determination and say, "I'll never lose that temper of mine again," or, "I'll never do that thing again; I loathe it." But we find ourselves back in the old atmosphere and the old company, and temptation comes with new and attractive garb. We find ourselves bound by sin again and our resolves lie shattered around us.

The prayer of a man yielded to the will of God is not for outward well-being, but for inward character, for deliverance from this repetition of sinning. He prays, not for better circumstances, but for greater likeness to Christ.

Every time a man slips up, he hates himself the more that he has fallen again and grieved his Lord. He knows that his business colleagues, his friends that are unconverted, or his family, look at him and say, "That's Christianity for you! I told you it would happen. You could never keep it up." He hides his face in shame as he goes to his own private room, kneeling by his bed and weeping with anguish and sorrow and remorse. "Oh, God, is there no answer to this sin in my life that constantly gets me down?"

No wonder this petition, "Lead us not into temptation," finds a place in our hearts daily. How we dread to meet the enemy, for we know how weak we are! Unless the Lord matches the onslaughts of the devil with His omnipotent strength, we will go on wallowing in the mire.

> Yield not to temptation,
>   For yielding is sin;
> Each victory will help you
>   Some other to win.

So goes a familiar hymn, but I'm sorry to say I cannot agree with it.

No victory over temptation makes us stronger than we were before. If we think it does, we shall fail. It was that false supposition which caused Joshua's armies to lose the battle of Ai after victory at Jericho. They thought that conquering Jericho had made them strong and that little Ai would be easy to overcome.

The fact is, Christian friends, that all through our lives every experience of conflict is given to teach us the lesson that ". . . in me, (that is, in my flesh), dwelleth no good thing. . . ." The moment the child of God begins to think that because he has got the victory once he will overcome sin the next time, he will go down. As one battles his way through temptation, he discovers his own desperate weakness, his own helplessness apart from the grace of God. He finds that the pathway which one avalanche of temptation has hollowed out in his life lies ready and waiting to receive the next attack. Therefore, unless the grace of God in omnipotent power blocks the

advance of Satan, the child of God will go down
again.

Must these things continue? No, thank God, He
answers our petition, "Lead us not into temptation."
But we need to understand the tactics used by the
enemy of our souls. We need to realize the true character of the warfare in which we are engaged, and to
understand the tremendous issues which are at stake.
This is a big subject, and I am but taking one little
phrase. We will also need to consider the second
part of it, "Deliver us from evil," to go into the true
spiritual warfare of the Christian. For a full study of
the subject I recommend to you Bunyan's *Holy War*.

First of all, let us consider the source of temptation.
The implication of "Lead us not into temptation" is
that God tempts His children, that He leads us into
circumstances which are calculated to trip us up. Is
that true?

James 1:13 says, "Let no man say when he is
tempted, I am tempted of God: for God cannot be
tempted with evil, neither tempteth he any man."
That seems to contradict the suggestion of the prayer
concerning the source of temptation. But Genesis
22:1 says, ". . . God did tempt Abraham, and said
unto him, . . . Take now thy son, . . . Isaac, . . .
and offer him . . . for a burnt-offering. . . ." Yet
again, in Matthew 4:1 we read, "Then was Jesus led
of the spirit into the wilderness to be tempted of the
devil."

No, there is no contradiction in these statements—
the truth is that temptation has two parts to it. First,

there are the circumstances which may or may not lead to sin. Then there is the desire within your life, the fifth columnist, if you like, who is aroused by those circumstances. Those two parts are operative in every temptation: the circumstances themselves which suddenly confront you, and which find that within you they have an ally, a Quisling, whom they address by proffering certain conditions.

You see, there must be tinder as well as spark if you are going to kindle a flame. If fire falls on water or bare rock, it won't kindle anything. It is God who sends the fire; it is you who light the flame. He tempts only insofar as He creates circumstances which are either an occasion for falling or an opportunity to prove His power to keep you.

In that sense, temptation is merely testing. I quote to you from the Apostle Peter, ". . . you, who are kept by the power of God through faith unto salvation ready to be revealed in the last time. Wherein ye greatly rejoice, though now for a season, if need be, ye are in heaviness through manifold temptations: that the trial of your faith, being much more precious than of gold that perisheth, though it be tried with fire, might be found unto praise and honour and glory at the appearing of Jesus Christ" (I Peter 1:4–7).

God permits temptation in our lives to prove the profession of our faith in Jesus Christ and to discipline our Christian character by teaching us to rely completely upon Him for power. God allowed Satan to sift Job, but first of all Satan had to ask God's permission. No temptation, testing, or trial is allowed to touch the life of God's child without God's permission, and He permits it in order to test our faith. Satan attacks to secure our downfall. God never in malice will tempt any of His children, but always in mercy He will try them. I trust that this brief explanation will bring some comfort or light upon the warfare in which you may be engaged.

But let me call your attention, in the second place, to the strength of temptation. It has no power at all apart from the personality of the devil. I do not know, of course, whether you believe in the personality of the devil. I do—I know him too well to doubt him. The more I love the Lord the more I hate the enemy. He who knows the Saviour best will also know Satan more perfectly. That is why, you see, this prayer is followed by "but deliver us from evil"—that is, "from the evil one."

Remember that temptation, in itself, is never sin. Jesus was tempted in all points like as we are, yet without sin. It is not the man who yields to temptation who knows its strength. Someone says, "That temptation was terribly strong. I went down so quickly!" That man knows nothing about temptation's power. But another will come and say, "I am being attacked; I am fighting a battle. This thing in my heart is too strong for me, but by the grace of God I am standing." That person is using the language of the Apostle Paul when he wrote to the church at Ephesus, "That you may be able to stand your ground in the evil day, and, having fought through to the end [or—and I love this

translation—"having been fought to a standstill"] remain victor on the field" (Ephesians 6:13, Weymouth). Do you know anything about that experience
in your life? Am I using language strange to you,
speaking of something quite out of the realm of your
experience, or are you at present being "fought to a
standstill"? Are there some places in your life where
you are not putting up, perhaps, the resistance you
ought? For the power of the devil in the Christian's life is known only by the man who, in the name
of the Lord Jesus Christ, is determined to stand his
ground.

"Lead us not into temptation" is the one negative
petition in the family prayer; it is the one thing we
dread more than anything else. I could paraphrase it
this way, and I often do as I seek the Lord myself:
"Lord, I am weak, and I would avoid every temptation of the devil if I could. I do not ask to be exempt
from trial, because that would not be good for me,
but, Lord, if today there is to be put in my path an
inducement to sin, Lord Jesus, then lead me through.
Take my hand, and keep me near to You, Lord Jesus.
I don't ask to be free from the furnace of testing, but,
O God, I desperately need Your presence through
the fire."

"But every man," says James, "is tempted, when
he is drawn away of his own lust, and enticed. Then
when lust hath conceived, it bringeth forth sin: and
sin, when it is finished, bringeth forth death" (James
1:14–15). That is the downward process. At the back
of it there is Satan, determined to destroy us.

Finally, I must say one word concerning the Saviour in temptation. Where does He come into all this? If God allows my life or your life to be tested almost beyond endurance, if He allows us to face situations where we are utterly "fought to a standstill," it is because He is able to keep us in any situation. He will never send His child into any situation from which He cannot save him. Listen to Paul's testimony to the church at Corinth: "There hath no temptation taken you but such as is common to man: but God is faithful, who will not suffer you to be tempted above that you are able; but will, with the temptation, also make a way of escape, that you may be able to bear it" (I Corinthians 10:13).

Hear also the words of Peter: "The Lord knoweth how to deliver the godly out of temptation" (II Peter 2:9). And, in the words of the writer of Hebrews 2:18: "In that he himself hath suffered being tempted, He is able to succour those that are tempted." Those words come like water to my thirsty heart. What sweet music they are in the heat of the battle! Because of this assurance, James says, "Count it all joy when you fall into divers temptations." Why? Because in them we prove the power of Christ, and we know that they are sent for a purpose. We cling to Him for deliverance, not from temptation, but from Satan.

There is no situation through which He will ask us to go except that in it He is able to save us completely. Does someone say to me that He doesn't save you like that? "I don't know anything about

victory. He doesn't give me power over temptation."

But tell me, Christian friend, are you really honest
when you pray that prayer? Excuse me for putting
it so bluntly, but you do not expect the Lord to
answer that prayer, do you, if you date someone who
is ruining your life? If you say, "Lord, lead me not
into temptation," and then, when you are on your
feet, you run directly to it, do not be surprised that
your prayer is not answered.

Do you pray, "Lead me not into temptation," and
then when you get out of the church you switch on
your television set to a play that is not quite decent?
Is your library full of books that ought to be burned?
If I pray, "Lord Jesus, lead me not into temptation,"
that prayer is going to decide the company I keep,
the books I read, the places I go, for I need never
expect Jesus Christ my Saviour to keep me from
temptation if I walk right into it.

If you will come to Jesus Christ in humility and
say to Him, "Lord, I want to cut out of my life everything that dims my vision of Thyself, everything that
makes my worship unreal. Lord Jesus, I want him
or her or it to go." If I am prepared to say that, then
I can look up into His face and add, "Lord, lead me
not into temptation," and He will take my hand. He
will see me through many deep waters, but they will
never overflow me; He will take me into many a
furnace, but the flame cannot touch me. Then one
day He will present me faultless before His throne
with exceeding joy.

Chapter VIII

Deliver Us From Evil

As we studied the phrase, "Lead us not into temptation," we saw the child of God, conscious of past sin and failure and fearful of falling into yet further sin, clinging to his Saviour. The next petition brings before us a different picture. Now we see the Christian as a warrior in the battle, conscious that the odds against him are too great and that he will go down unless he receives help from a power infinitely greater than himself.

What a picture of need we see in this second part of the Lord's prayer! "Give us this day our daily bread"—hunger. "Forgive us our debts—sin. "Lead us not into temptation"—weakness. And now that dreadful, all-inclusive word that sums up everything —"Deliver us from *evil*." Against powerful adversaries the child of God prays for forgiveness, for protection, and for deliverance. Each step in this prayer seems to take him further into the darkness until he comes to this desperate cry which takes within its scope every ill to which the human heart can ever be prey, "Deliver us, O Lord, from evil!"

We know that if we ask anything according to His will He heareth us, and therefore this is not only a prayer, but a prophecy. For surely our Lord taught us to pray, "Our Father, deliver us from evil" because it was in His will to do so. In the midst of the battle and conflict of Christian living the Lord Jesus Christ Himself plants this living hope in the heart of each one of His own—the hope that one day He shall break every yoke, snap every fetter, burst every chain, remove every burden, and set His people free. Therefore, though in a sense we touch here the greatest depths of human need, we rise to the greatest heights of Christian faith and confidence in God.

Notice the unlimited scope of this petition, "Deliver us from evil." The more I meditate on it the more conscious I become of the vastness and the inclusiveness of this prayer. I recommend again that you read Bunyan's *Holy War* page by page and line by line to see the true nature of the battle in which we are engaged.

What does this word "evil" mean? We generally use it to describe two distinct and separate things, one of them internal and the other external. One has to do with character and the other with circumstance; the one with sin and the other with sorrow. There is in all our lives what we call physical evil: pain, sorrow, everything that destroys our happiness. There is also what we call moral evil, everything that wars against our longings for character, purity, and goodness.

Certainly it is useless to persuade a man to believe that he is not suffering when his body is wracked with pain, or when his heart is broken. There is no part of human life which has not been blighted by evil. It is evil to be in pain. It is evil to be crushed by sorrow. It is evil to watch a hole in the ground swallow a coffin containing the earthly remains of someone who has been the joy of our heart. It is evil for the arrows of hate or bitterness or jealousy to wound our spirit. It is evil to toil at a task that is beyond our strength. This whole human life, which turns the sweet, pure, face of a child into the wizened, wrinkled, careworn, anxious face of age, this life which changes the light step of childhood into the slow, heavy tread of an old man, is sin and evil. From beginning to end it is evil!

These things are all external, but the dominion of evil within our hearts that is contrary to the will of God lies deeper still. The will of God takes in our holiness as well as our happiness. Whether by means of chastening and discipline, or by grace, mercy, and the out-streaming of God's love—all the resources of heaven are directed to prepare each one of us to stand faultless before the throne in the image of Jesus Christ, the image which man lost when he rebelled against his God.

Our holiness and our happiness—the two are inextricably entwined together. No man can be truly happy until the Spirit of God has mastered the legion of devils that are within him. No man can have a moment's peace until he has found peace with God by the blood of the cross. Then he will discover the peace of God standing day by day like a sentinel, guarding him from the attacks of the evil one. No man can taste real happiness until he has received that fountain of life within him that springs up into everlasting life.

So ceaselessly does the Spirit war against the flesh, and the flesh against the Spirit, that we cannot do the things that we would. Therefore, when we cry, "Lord, deliver us from evil!" we are saying (as the word really means), "O Lord, rescue us!" We are like men and women who are drowning, who have been overcome by the tempest and flood. We are in imminent danger of death and disaster unless someone comes to our rescue and saves us.

I repeat, there is no part of life which is not touched by evil. It has ruined our circumstances, it has marred our character, it has affected the whole of God's lovely creation, for, says Paul in Romans 8:22–23, ". . . the whole creation groaneth and travaileth in pain together until now. And not only they, but ourselves also, which have the first-fruits of the Spirit, even we ourselves groan within ourselves, waiting for the adoption, to wit the redemption of our body."

Therefore this prayer recognizes evil as a deadly fact. The New Testament is utterly opposed to that theory which tries to argue that fire will not burn, and pain will not kill, and sin will not destroy. Christianity faces the fact of human suffering; Christ wept over it, and He bade the daughters of Jerusalem weep over it also.

Certainly our Christian faith has much to say about suffering and evil being for our good; about submission to the will of God being better than the panic-stricken efforts to get out of it immediately. But the Bible declares that evil *is* evil. Job, you remember, was tormented by the pious platitudes of his friends, who held up their hands in holy horror because he refused to accept his dunghill as a bed of roses. Job was sure that God was good, and he was equally sure that pain was bad, and though he could not reconcile the two he refused to be shaken from his conviction.

When we say, "Lord, deliver us from evil," we find the limitless breadth of that prayer covering everything that makes our bodies ache and our hearts break and our consciences guilty and sore. There is no boundary to the evil which has gripped this world. There is no limit to the evil which has gripped our hearts and molested our lives. Evil is the thing against which we Christians battle every day of our experience.

But in the second place this petition reveals the unity and source of evil. We have described evil from two different angles, but at root it is one. Like some monster of imagination which has a hundred heads, it has but one heart. When I pray, "Deliver me from evil," I am in fact praying, "O God, deliver me from *the evil one."* If we can recognize the true nature of our warfare and the character of our enemy, we will be stronger to face him. At the bottom of all evil is the person of Satan.

Satan is revealed in his true colors in the Word of God. "How art thou fallen from heaven, O Lucifer, son of the morning! . . . For thou hast said in thine heart, I will ascend into heaven, I will exalt my throne above the stars of God . . . I will be like the most High. Yet thou shalt be brought down to hell . . ." (Isaiah 14:12–15).

That is Satan, the leader of rebellion in the very courts of heaven, the ambitious usurper of the very glory of God. One day not only in this world, which is but the battlefield, but in all the universe, the glory of God will be revealed supremely in the man whom God has made in His likeness to be His ruler over this world. Therefore all of Satan's attacks are concentrated on mankind, not primarily to destroy us, but in order that by the destruction of man he might rob God of all His glory.

He achieved an initial triumph when he succeeded in dragging the human race into sin against their Creator and God. It was not final, for the Bible tells us that the glory of God in redemption at the cross exceeded the glory that He had in creation, for into the sacrifice of Jesus of Nazareth, the Christ of God, upon a tree, God the Father has woven the rich and glorious pattern of the gospel of His grace. Because of that we now know, as we could never otherwise have known, how much He loves us, how He was prepared to pay any price to win us back to Himself. The cross has demonstrated how He was prepared to empty heaven of all its wealth of glory, to give Himself, down to the last drop of His blood, indeed, to pay the price of saving humanity from ruin and disaster, to win us back from the power of Satan.

But it is still Satan's aim to frustrate God's purpose of grace. Heaven's objective is to display the glory of God in redeemed humanity; Satan's fiendish, foul purpose is to destroy it in broken humanity (and you do not have to go far in any big city to discover how successful he is!). The ultimate, eternal purpose of God, I repeat, is that Christ might be admired in all them that believe. The greatest glory of heaven for the eternal ages is the "bride adorned to meet her husband"—the family of God ransomed, healed, restored, forgiven, with the Lamb of God upon the throne.

On the other hand, Satan's ultimate design is to blot out every trace of the image of God upon humanity, to bring about man's eternal ruin in order to show himself more powerful than the omnipotent God! As we read in Weymouth's translation of Ephesians 6:11: "Ours is not a conflict with mere flesh and blood, but with the despotisms, the empires, the forces that control and govern this dark world, the spiritual hosts of evil arrayed against us in this heavenly warfare."

This is but a glimpse into the true nature and source of all evil, and of the battle which we fight. Earth is the battlefield, and your personality and mine are the focal points upon which God and Satan are directing all their forces, Satan to blind and ruin you and to land you in a Christless hell; Jesus to save and mold you and to make you holy, pure and good that one day He may be admired in you.

My fellow Christians, have you ever stopped to think of the nature of the spiritual battle in which you are engaged? If we had, I feel many of us would take this Christian life more seriously than we do. Many of us would recognize that every day our lives are being molded and shaped: that Satan is attacking, and that God the Holy Spirit is here to give power and strength to resist him. We would realize that we cannot afford to play with sin. We cannot afford to live this Christian life on the circumference of reality. We are engaged in a desperate battle against powerful forces, and therefore every day we have to cry, "Lord, deliver us from evil!"

Where else could we turn for help and strength? Against all the onslaught of inward sin and external sorrow, both coming, indeed, from the same source, God delivers from both character and circumstance by the same mighty Saviour, the Lord Jesus Christ.

He delivers us from sin by answering every petition of this family prayer. When I say to Him honestly and earnestly, "My Father," claiming my relationship through faith in Jesus Christ; when I bow before Him and say, "Hallowed be Thy name" in every part of my life; when I say, "Thy kingdom come"—reign Thou in me; when I pray, "Thy will be done, Lord, in my life today"—when I pray these things and I mean them, then every moment of my life there is fresh grace to meet every need. There is fresh cleansing to meet every sin. There is fresh power to meet every temptation, and there is a mighty God who Himself has overcome our enemy at the empty tomb and risen triumphantly above—our Deliverer from every sin.

He also delivers us from every suffering and sorrow. The Lord teaches His children through many different circumstances that ". . . all things work together for good to them that love (Him). . . ." Sometimes He chooses to take his child *out* of suffering almost immediately. Sometimes he chooses to let His child remain *in* it for a lifetime, but always He takes him *through* it. And finally He is going to deliver us from evil by taking us home to Himself.

This prayer reaches far beyond the depth of human need and experience and expresses the yearning in our hearts for complete redemption. It is the last prayer of all that God will ever answer. It reveals to us that the day will come when His name shall be hallowed everywhere, His kingdom set up in perfect righteousness, His will done on earth universally. Our every want shall be supplied, our every sin forgiven, our every temptation overcome, and the evil one put away in chains.

This petition, "Deliver us from evil" is being answered every day of our Christian lives in constant mercy and gracious guidance, but it will be completely answered only when all His people stand united before the throne. Surely one of the most wonderful sentences in the whole Bible is the one which tells us that God *Himself* shall wipe away every tear. There are some things He delegates to angels, there are other things that He can entrust to men, but the healing of broken hearts and the wiping of tear-stained faces is a task which God Himself will do. "And God shall wipe away all tears from their eyes; and there shall be no more death, neither sorrow, nor crying, neither shall there be any more pain: for the former things are passed away" (Revelation 21:4).

Out of the midst of the battle, as we tune our hearts with heaven, seeking in the Word of God to understand some of the mysteries of sorrow and trouble, and the source of all evil, as we know some of that internal battle and conflict of soul with the enemy, how wonderful it is to realize that some day the noise of battle will be merely as the sound of some distant sea breaking on the shore. One day it will be only a memory of a tremendous storm that broke, for every wind will be silenced and all will be calm.

We pray for that day to come: "Lord, deliver us from evil!"

> Christian, dost thou see them
>   On the holy ground,
> How the powers of darkness
>   Compass thee around?
> Christian, up and smite them,
>   Counting gain but loss;
> Smite them by the merit
>   Of the holy cross.

Christian, dost thou feel them,
How they work within,
Striving, tempting, luring,
Goading into sin?
Christian, never tremble,
Never be downcast;
Gird thee for the conflict,
Watch and pray and fast.

Christian, dost thou hear them,
How they speak thee fair?
'Always fast and vigil?
Always watch and prayer?'
Christian, answer boldly,
'While I breathe I pray';
Peace shall follow battle,
Night shall end in day.

'Well I know thy trouble,
O my servant true;
Thou art very weary—
I was weary too;
But that toil shall make thee
Some day all Mine own,
And the end of sorrow
Shall be near My throne.'

                              Andrew of Crete
                              tr. by J. M. Neale

Chapter IX

Thine Is the Kingdom

We come now to consider the doxology of the family prayer. This pattern of all praying began in worship, continued in intercession, and concludes in praise. There is so much treasure to be dug out of this doxology that we shall need more than one study to mine it.

First, let us think of what it means really to praise God. What are the characteristics of praise? Then we will look at the ascription of praise here, *"Thine* is the kingdom," and finally we will consider the implications of praise as they affect us personally.

Praise is an essential element in all real praying. Consider the petitions of the family prayer, for instance—when we pray, "Give us this day our daily bread," we magnify the goodness of God. When we pray for His forgiveness, we exalt His mercy. When we ask for guidance, "Lead us not into temptation," we honor His wisdom and His power. When we pray for deliverance from all evil, we are extolling His strength.

Praise has been the thread which runs through all the depths of want and need expressed in this prayer. We may not always recognize it because we are so deeply conscious of our immediate needs. When we come before God and open our hearts to Him, when we let Him know just what our need is, then we praise Him. For there is nothing that brings more joy even to the heart of God than to hear the cry from some soul, "God, be merciful to me, a sinner."

Praise is based upon sound argument, surely. We say, "For Thine is the kingdom," and we expect God to hear us and to meet our need, not because of anything in ourselves, but because of His promises. Our hope and our confidence are in God when we pray—in His character, His name, His authority, His promises. It is not even our faith nor our helplessness upon which we base our plea, but rather His kingdom, His power, His glory. When we truly pray, the foundation of all our hope and confidence is in God alone.

When out of the depths we begin to praise God, we do so because we know that His name, His glory, and His promises are all linked inseparably with the need of our hearts. The glory of God is at stake in our salvation; the character of God is concerned about our holiness and happiness; the promise of God is linked with the supply of our every need in Christ Jesus our Lord. Therefore praise is the foundation of all our praying, for faith itself is praise. In our extremity and need, and often in desperation, faith lifts its heart to God, begins to contemplate the character of God, His holiness, His love, His promises; and then faith, having contemplated God, begins to appropriate all the infinite resources of God that are ours in Jesus Christ our Lord. Praise, I say, is an essential element in all our praying.

Not only is praise an expression of faith in God's ability to do something for us here and now; it is also an anticipation of all that God has in store for His people. "Thine is the kingdom, and the power and the glory *forever*." The Lord Jesus Christ stood at the tomb of Lazarus while he was yet dead and prayed, ". . . Father, I thank thee that thou hast heard me." So in the midst of life's difficulties we also are lifted above every sorrow and every inward conflict of soul when we can lose ourselves in rejoicing with Him in anticipation of the day when we shall be joining in the songs of angels around the throne of God. Praise, therefore, is not only faith to believe that God can meet my need now, but it is a wonderful anticipation of what God has in store for those who trust Him.

How precious is the praise of our God! This new song, this breath of the Holy Spirit, this voice of the living Christ in the Church, the undercurrent of all our praying, the argument behind our every request, the anticipation of heaven: "Whoso offereth praise glorifieth the Lord." What a precious thing it is to praise God like that!

But let us think for a moment concerning the ascription of praise in the family prayer. "*Thine* is the kingdom, and the power and the glory." We are going to consider now only the first of these three: "Thine is the kingdom." What do we mean when we say that? The Word of God teaches that there is a visible and material kingdom, and there is an invisible, spiritual kingdom. As to the first, we read of a kingdom of darkness and a kingdom of light, but strictly speaking there are not two kingdoms, or two kings: "Thine *is* the kingdom."

"The earth is the Lord's and the fulness thereof," says the Psalmist, "the world, and they that dwell therein" (Psalm 24:1). ". . . the Lord God omnipotent (not *shall* reign, but *does* reign) reigneth" (Revelation 19:6). "Thine is the kingdom"—a present, blessed, wonderful experience today. Jesus is not going to be King, He *is* King now. As the nobleman of whom He spoke in Luke 19, who went into a far country to receive for himself a kingdom and to return, so the Lord Jesus Christ has received the kingdom. Some people seem to think that God has lost control of this world and that He now is planning a great campaign to reconquer the sovereignty of the world which has got out of His hands. But that is not the teaching of the Word of God. Satan may be prince of this world, and it may be in revolt against the authority of God—certainly much in it offends and grieves Him. There may be tares and weeds, but they will be burned; there may be rebels against God, but they will be banished!

"Thine *is* the kingdom."

Let me illustrate from a contemporary event in history. King George VI of Britain went to London Airport early in 1953 to say good-by to his daughter and her husband as they went to tour the Commonwealth. He never saw them again: a few weeks later he died. When the announcement of his death was made, there followed immediately the public proclamation of Elizabeth as Queen. And as she stepped from her plane the following morning, having returned from Kenya Colony, she was the acknowledged Queen of her people; she had already been acclaimed queen, and had received the kingdom. It was hers by right. Eighteen months later, however, she was crowned, and on that day, which attracted the interest of the whole world, her subjects knelt before her, in the persons of their representatives, and accepted her sovereignty. Before Elizabeth II on her coronation day every knee of every subject bowed in willing submission, and they crowned her Queen.

Christian friends, Jesus Christ is King! Today He is King by right. His death and resurrection have robbed Satan of every claim to supremacy. But the coronation day is coming. One day Jesus shall be crowned; before Him every knee shall bow! He is King by sovereign right now, but one day the whole world will bow before Him in submission, acknowledging His supremacy and Lordship.

Rejoice! the Lord is King;
   Your Lord and King adore;
Mortals, give thanks and sing,
   And triumph evermore:

Jesus the Saviour reigns,
   The God of truth and love;
When He had purged our stains,
   He took His seat above:

His kingdom cannot fail:
   He rules o'er earth and heaven;
The keys of death and hell
   Are to our Jesus given:

Lift up your heart, lift up your voice:
Rejoice; again I say, rejoice.
                              —Charles Wesley

As we think of this ascription of praise when we
pray the family prayer. "Thine is the kingdom," we
are acknowledging a fact, a present-day reality, that
Jesus our Lord is King, and we are anticipating a
crowning day when before Him every knee shall bow.
It is that tremendous truth which gives all history
meaning and purpose. The kingdom of God is over
all, and we wait for the manifestation of that kingdom when He shall come.

Meantime it is not the laws of the devil or of
hell which operate in this world, but the law of
heaven itself. For the Lord Jesus Christ overrules

everything for His glory. All human powers and empires, though they may not realize it, are operating together to fulfill His eternal purpose. Though men may not do it wittingly, yet they cannot avoid serving the ultimate purpose of God. In this world of ours, wracked with trouble and danger and disaster, it is not Satan who is in charge; it is our God who is upon the throne. It is not the powers of darkness that rule; it is the power of the kingdom of light and glory, far above all principality and power: Jesus our Lord is upon the throne! Only then does modern, contemporary history make sense.

There is not only a visible and material kingdom, but there is a spiritual kingdom also. ". . . the kingdom of God is not meat and drink; but righteousness, and peace, and joy in the Holy Ghost" (Romans 14: 17). In that kingdom Jesus is also King. The gates of that kingdom are praise, and the walls of it are salvation. It is protected and defended against all its enemies, and within that kingdom He gives to His servants a place of work, a place of service. He distributes His gifts and powers according to His own pleasure.

It is only those who taste the joys of this spiritual kingdom who will share one day in the authority of His physical kingdom. ". . . Except a man be born from above," said the Lord Jesus Christ, "he cannot see the kingdom of God." By virtue of a new birth, by the regenerating power of the Holy Spirit we become members of this invisible spiritual kingdom. Then He begins to prepare and train us for service in that visible kingdom, when the inward fruits of righteousness, joy, and peace in the Spirit of God shall be expressed in every relationship throughout the world. If you and I are members of that spiritual kingdom today, and are expressing through our lives that righteousness, joy, and peace in the Holy Spirit, we are but anticipating the experience which will be world-wide when, in the visible kingdom of God, these qualities will become universal.

"Thine is the kingdom": the kingdom of visible power, and the kingdom of invisible spiritual reality: Jesus Christ is Lord over them both.

But most important of all are the implications of this praise. Truth must have its impact upon each one of us if it is to be of value. It is the letter of the law which kills; it is the Spirit which gives life.

When our praying is praise, when there is this new song in our heart, what then? Surely it draws together, as nothing else can, Christian people in love to God, in love to Jesus Christ, and in love to each other. It is this "shout of the King," this triumphant note of victory in the Christian Church which drives out discord and brings in harmony. When we give to God the praise that is His due, we acknowledge that He is to be at the center of everything. And when God is at the center, self is destroyed, and love begins to reign.

The secret of every discord which exists in Christian homes and Christian communities and Christian churches is that we seek our own way and our own glory. Too often do we praise men, and too seldom do we praise God. Too often do we recognize human achievements, and too seldom do we acknowledge the power of God. Self can come in so many forms and guises. It may take the form of a particular creed or doctrine, which may be correct and valuable, but when doctrine is at the center of a church, and takes the place that Christ ought to have, you may be sure of a divided church.

True praise draws us all together, as one in Jesus Christ our Lord. How much of that quality of praise is there in us—praise which gives all glory to Him; praise which throws everything at the Master's feet; service which seeks no recognition.

It was C. H. Spurgeon, I think, who one day after a morning service was confronted by a lady who said to him, "Mr. Spurgeon, that was a wonderful sermon you preached this morning."

"Yes, ma'am," he said, "the devil told me that ten minutes ago."

What we need in our churches today—urgently, desperately—is not that people should come to hear a preacher, and then tell him what a good (or bad) sermon he preached, but that they should leave the house of God saying, "What a wonderful Lord!" When all praise is given to Him and taken from man, a church rises in spiritual temperature and becomes irresistible.

But in a more personal way still, when we say, "Thine is the kingdom," we acknowledge that you and I are the subjects of the King! Have you been born into this kingdom? Do you know the fruit of the kingdom in your experience: righteousness, joy, and peace in the Holy Spirit? Is it not true of some of us that we constantly seek to establish our own righteousness and to boast of our own achievements? The throne of our heart, then, is occupied by the puppet of "self." While it is true that Jesus is King according to our lips, in truth and in practice do we act in utter contradiction to Him? Do we acknowledge His right of sovereignty, Christian friends, but are not crowning Him in our lives? We say, "Thine is the kingdom"; we trust Him and receive Him as our Saviour. We believe that He indwells our hearts by the Holy Spirit. In theory He is King, but let me ask you, in practice, who is running your life?

I remember visiting a town in the midlands of England where they make pottery—a dirty, smoky place called Stoke-on-Trent, where I heard of a man, very illiterate, who had been living a very bad sort of life. But one day he received Christ at a Salvation Army meeting, and showed he was truly converted.

One Sunday morning he came home from the Salvation Army's holiness meeting very miserable.

"What's the matter with you?" asked his wife. "I thought you said you'd got converted."

"I am," he said, "but I'm so miserable today because everyone had red jerseys on but me."

"Oh," replied his wife, "that's easy. I'll knit you one!"

So she sat down and knitted him a red jersey that week, and the next Sunday he went to the meeting proudly wearing it. He came back home miserable.

"What's the matter with you now?" asked his puzzled wife.

"Well, you see," he said, "everybody else had some lovely white letters on their red jerseys, but I had none."

"What can we do about that?" wondered his wife. "What are we going to put on it?" The poor woman couldn't read, either, so she didn't know what to do. As she sat down at her window, she noticed that across the street a store had put up a new banner, so she decided to copy the letters and sew them on her husband's jersey.

The next Sunday morning he came home radiant!

"Do you know, my dear," he said, "everybody said that I had the best jersey of anyone there!"

Do you know what was written on it? "Under new management!"

Are you "under new management"? Is Jesus Christ King in practice as well as in theory? Is the kingdom of your personality His? Has He had a coronation day in your heart?

"Thine is the kingdom," we say, and yet—

"She is *my* friend," we assert, "and I will not give her up."

"That is *my* home," we claim, "and everything in it belongs to me."

"This is *my* money, and I'm holding on to it! It is *my* business, and it must not be interfered with."

"It is *my* life," we say, "and I will run it for myself."

It is not the unbeliever who talks like that always; frequently it is the child of God. It is the Christian who in theory crowns Christ King, and acknowledges His right to rule, but in terms of six days a week's daily conduct talks of "*my* friend, *my* home, *my* business, *my* money," and God is not in them.

The strange thing about it—and yet not so strange because it reveals a great truth—is that when in practice we go on saying, "my," none of these things are ours at all to enjoy. But when we can honestly look up into His face and say, "Lord Jesus Christ, I crown Thee Lord of all. I freely acknowledge Thy Lordship not merely in theory, but I put the crown upon Thy brow and fall at Thy feet. From this moment onward I am Thy slave and Thy servant— I am all Thine, every part of the kingdom of my personality is Thine." When I say that, then all these other things are truly mine. For they cannot be truly mine until I possess them in Jesus Christ.

A little child will say of his birthday gift, "This is *my* toy." He walks up the street from school with his playmates and points, "That is *my* house." He hears a heavier, familiar step on the front walk, looks out the window, then rushes to the front door and cries, "*My* Daddy!" But he did not earn the toy; he did not buy the house; he did not purchase his father. They were all his by gift!

When I look up into His face and say, "Thine, Lord Jesus, is the kingdom," then I can say, "Lord, he (or she) is my friend, because he is Thy gift to me." He is mine because he is His.

Can I say, "If Thou art in my amusements, my recreation, my fun, my money, Lord Jesus, then they are mine. If Thou art not in them, then they are not mine."

If you think about it for a moment, honestly, that statement will answer every problem you may ever have concerning what you call worldly amusements. They are yours if He is in them. If He is not in them, then they are not yours. Otherwise His is not the kingdom. And if you are in doubt, give God the benefit of the doubt and cut it out. Let it be true from the depths of your heart to the circumference of your life, "Thine is the kingdom."

Christian friends, is He Lord in theory only, or in practice also?

> Lord of every thought and action,
>   Lord to send, and Lord to stay,
> Lord in speaking, writing, giving,
>   Lord in all things to obey;
> Lord of all there is of me,
> Now and evermore to be.

Chapter X

The Power and the Glory

In this chapter we are continuing the doxology of the family prayer, "Thine is the kingdom, the power, and the glory forever." We shall come to the conclusion of our study in the next chapter when we think together about the "Amen." This wonderful doxology of praise crowns the worship and intercession of the prayer and expresses the conviction that every petition in it will be answered. Its confidence is based upon the solid argument of God's supreme authority and power.

At the same time, when we conclude this family prayer by saying, "Thine is the kingdom, the power, and the glory forever," that statement searches out every hidden motive in our praying. It tests our sincerity to the utmost.

"Thine is the kingdom" was our subject in the last chapter. We compared the material, visible kingdom of God with the spiritual, invisible kingdom of God within us, and we saw that the Lord is King in both. As we experience His Lordship in the spiritual kingdom of righteousness, joy, and peace in the Holy Spirit, as we know Him in His indwelling power and control day by day, so we shall reign with Him one day in the visible kingdom, which is now His by right, and which at His return He will establish.

But now we are going to think for just a little while about this tremendous statement, "Thine is the power and the glory forever," in the light of personal Christian experience. We are going to be very practical. First we will look at the demonstration of the power and the glory of God in the Word of God. And then I must speak to you, I am afraid, concerning the denial of the power and glory of God in the church. And finally we will consider the diffusion of the power and glory of God through all eternity.

When we pray, "Thine is the power and the glory forever," we are merely giving assent to the greatest fact of the Word of God. "Power belongeth unto God," said David. "God hath spoken once; twice have I heard this; that power belongeth unto God" (Psalm 62:11). I imagine David meant that God had spoken directly to his heart, and told him that "power belongeth unto Me." And then that the spoken word found confirmation in the experiences of his life when he saw evidences that "power belongeth unto God."

That thought could be intensely shattering and

crushing if we did not understand that not only does power belong to God, but mercy also. If the power of God were not inseparably linked with the mercy of God, we would be desperately afraid. But the greatest manifestation of the power of God in the Book—and also of His mercy—is its revelation in Jesus Christ, especially in His death upon the cross for our sins.

From the very beginning to the end of His earthly life, the power of God was demonstrated in a remarkable way. It was shown, first of all, in renunciation. "He counted it not a thing to be grasped after," says the Apostle Paul, "to be equal with God, but he made himself of no reputation, and took upon him the form of a servant, and was made in the likeness of man. . . . he humbled himself and became obedient unto death, even the death of the cross" (Philippians 2:5–8).

Those tremendous downward steps of the ladder brought the eternal Son of God down into time, lower and lower and lower in renunciation of all His glory and all His rights—what a revelation of the power of God! And in order to support this demonstration of His power in a way which we could all understand, the New Testament records how a star shone along the road to lead the Wise Men to Bethlehem, and that the decree of Caesar Augustus to tax the whole world was in fulfillment of the prophecy made hundreds of years previously concerning the birthplace of Christ.

In the course of His earthly life all human power combined against Him—the traitor in His own camp, the high priests of the temple, Herod the king, Pilate the judge, the authority of the Roman Empire. They had their way with Him, apparently. They put Him in a grave and they guarded His tomb when He was silent and dead. But in the stillness of the night and without any human witness, God raised Him from the power of death. He was lifted up to the throne on high, and the power of God that was seen in renunciation was seen thereafter in resurrection authority and glory.

Then came that great outflow of the power of God which has continued ever since: that silent voice of the Holy Spirit began to speak to human hearts. That gentle touch which opened the heart of Lydia at the riverside, and has opened the hearts of thousands since then, is the demonstration of the power of God in regeneration.

All through the life of the Lord Jesus Christ, the supreme revelation of the power of God is seen, first, in the renunciation of His every right; second, in resurrection from the tomb to the throne; third, in the regeneration of human hearts: renunciation, resurrection, regeneration. The mighty, omnipotent power of God is still working silently, surely, without fuss or excitement, to reach multitudes of hearts.

Because the power is His, the glory is His also. Man has no part in His great demonstration of power in redeeming us, therefore man has no share in the glory and no credit for himself. It was all divinely conceived and divinely executed in the face of satanic opposition and human enmity. When Jesus came, He had no ally on earth to help Him—no ally in world conditions for the world was in utter darkness. He had no ally in the type of men He chose as His disciples—they were not brilliant intellects, they were not clever psychologists, they were merely fishermen and ordinary working people. He had no ally in the human heart, for His every approach to human nature was greeted by the enemy within the heart of all men, for the natural heart is at enmity with God. When He came to redeem us and to save us, all the power and all the glory were His; we had no share in it.

Therefore when we pray, "Thine is the power and the glory," we know that no darkness or disaster or catastrophe in world affairs can ever affect the eternal power of God. It is forever! No power can touch His omnipotence, and no human vainglory can ever match the glory of our God. God's paths have always been invisible. God's step has always been silent. No human ear can hear His voice, but His power is such that He could bring twelve legions to His aid if He wished. His power sent the ravens to feed a tried, lonely servant of His who was exhausted in his ministry. The invincible, invisible power of God, silently, simply, surely moves in the hearts of men. All the power and all the glory are His!

Yes, the greatest demonstration of the power of God was in this mighty, matchless plan of redemption for you in Jesus Christ our Saviour and our Lord.

But I must say, also, with a deep conviction in my own heart, that the church of the twentieth century, by her program and by her practice and by her principles, is denying the power and the glory of God. Therefore God cannot bless us. We assent to these truths when we pray, "Thine is the kingdom, and the power and the glory," but we deny them in our actions.

Reflect for a moment with me on the situation in New Testament times. The early church found herself, immediately after Pentecost, linked with all the power of omnipotence. Therefore she became a channel of the power of God. We see them waiting for ten days before God. We see them witnessing before men. We see them winning through in the battle against the powers of darkness. They prayed, and so effective was their praying that the very house in which they knelt was shaken by a great wind. The promise that was given to them was, ". . . ye shall receive power, after that the Holy Ghost is come upon you, and ye shall be witnesses unto me . . ." (Acts 1:8). They attempted not one single thing for God until they had received the promise and the fire had come; heaven had been opened and the Holy Spirit was upon them.

The power of God operated in the early church in exactly the same way as it operated in Jesus Christ. It was the power of God in renunciation with Him— He forsook His glory and made Himself of no reputation, and I notice in the testimony of the early church following their first great miracle, that with the crowd falling at their feet and worshiping them, Peter says, ". . . why look ye so earnestly on us, as though by our own power or holiness we had made this man to walk?" (Ac⁺s 3:12).

The whole principle of the testimony of the early church was that when they saw blessing they humbled themselves and looked up and said, "Lord, Thine is the power and Thine is the glory." When other people were converted, they went back to pray and to thank God that He had ever deigned to use such unworthy instruments. It was the principle of renunciation. The early church refused to touch the glory which belonged to Him, and because they refused to touch the glory God poured out the blessing.

It was power not only in renunciation, it was power also in resurrection. One of the most remarkable chapters in the Word of God concerning the Christian ministry is II Corinthians 4, and in the course of that chapter Paul writes, ". . . we which live are alway delivered unto death for Jesus' sake, that the life also of Jesus might be made manifest in our body. . . . death worketh in us, but life in you." They refused to touch the glory; they refused to take the credit, and because of that the risen life of an omnipotent Christ was revealed through them. This was the principle of resurrection. They died to any praise or commendation or credit, and then they lived only for the glory of God and for the honor of Jesus Christ. God could trust those people with an outpouring of the Holy Spirit because they gave back all the glory to Him.

It was power, therefore, in regeneration. Upon a ministry like that and to a church like that, inevitably there followed evidences of supernatural power. The story of the Acts of the Apostles is not meant to be exceptional; it is meant to be God's norm for the church. The principle which they oberved was simply this: daily dying on the part of the Christian leads to daily life on the part of the unconverted. The disciples died unto themselves and the sinners lived unto God.

My Christian friends, remember that these are the eternal laws of the Spirit of life in Christ. The Holy Spirit does not work in a casual fashion—He has principles and rules which are eternal: they are here in the Book for us all to see. And the law of the Spirit of life in Christ is this: if I die, men will live. If I give Him the glory, He will come down with power. If I take the credit and the praise for myself, and seek commendation from men, then heaven is shut, and the world is hardened, and my service is empty.

As I mention these things, I honestly hang my head before God in shame. These principles of life, this law of the Spirit, seem much too costly for twentieth-century Christendom. The terms of self-discipline are far too hard, and therefore the power has gone from us.

In place of the outpouring of the Spirit of God for power we substitute programs, personality, eloquence —all these things, our talents and our abilities, we present to the world as if to say, "Come and see our eloquence, our oratory, our church." On our knees we still say, "Thine is the power and the glory," but all our methods contradict it.

Things have happened spiritually in the capital of the British Empire recently that have not been known in history, and the only explanation that anybody can give is this: that at last God found a preacher with no special gift, but a man who was prepared to give Him all the credit and all the glory and all the praise, who refused to touch one little bit of it for himself, and the power of God fell upon the people.

We say, "Thine is the glory," but if we do not get a bit for ourselves, we resign. And we seek to do by committee procedure what can only be done by crucified prayer. By that I mean praying which turns aside every other concern, and which is so desperate that it refuses to let go until God blesses.

The disciples waited and the power came. We do not wait, and the power does not come. The disciples witnessed unto Him—we witness to our program, and the program becomes an awful burden. We speak to others of our talent and our ability, and we lose the battle.

It is impossible for me to get alongside you each one personally—God knows how much I wish I could, but I would urge upon you to wait upon God until you know again His power in your own soul. I urge upon you to refuse to plan a program until you ask yourself, "Can the world see anything about me to commend Him to others?"

D. L. Moody was told, "The world has yet to see what God can do through a man fully yielded to Him." And the world has yet to see what God can do through a church or a Christian who refuses to take the glory to themselves. Oh, that God would give us crucified men in the leadership of our churches, in every part of the work, on every committee! May everyone who has any voice of authority be a man who has died to his reputation, a man who is dead to himself, a man who can look up to the Father and say, "Thine is the kingdom—Thine shall be the power; Thine shall be the glory."

Christian friends, it is the costly way I am taking you. Today people seem to imagine that if you shout loudly and make enough noise you can get a crowd and that is power. I say to you with all my heart that God works silently. Stillness and quietness are the evidence of strength.

I am praying with all my heart that you and I might come the way of death, the way of crucifixion, the way of the cross, in which we care not for our position or our prestige, in which we cease to mind if we are not asked to take a prominent part in the work, in which we do not expect to be praised or recognized by men, in which we count praise and blame as nothing, in which we press on regardless of public favor or public hate, in which we go through with the eternal counsel and will of God regardless of the praise or blame of mankind, in which we desire only to see the Lord Jesus Christ working in our lives, and to say to Him, "Thine is the power and Thine is the glory."

So much of the twentieth-century approach to evangelism seems to be program, popularity, talent, and ability, instead of prayer, humility, sacrifice, and glory to God. He will not give His glory to another, and He will not anoint with power a human nature that is satisfied with its own programs. But if we can have leadership in our churches that knows what it is to die to popularity and programs, then the power of the Third Person of the Trinity will blaze upon us once again in revival blessing.

"Is it worth it?" someone may say to me here. "All this sounds to me like a very uninteresting sort of plan."

It is not ours to choose, but God's purpose is the diffusion of the power and glory of God through all eternity. The truth is this—and I give it to you in the words of the Bible—". . . other foundation can no man lay than that is laid, which is Jesus Christ. . . . if any man build upon this foundation gold, silver, precious stones, wood, hay stubble; every man's work shall be made manifest: for the day shall declare it because it shall be revealed by fire; and the fire shall try every man's work, of what sort it is. If any man's work shall abide, . . . he shall receive a reward. If any man's work shall be burned, he shall suffer loss: but he himself shall be saved; yet so as by fire" (I Corinthians 3:11–15).

There is an awful judgment awaiting the world that has rejected Christ. I believe there is also a judgment awaiting the Christian who has refused the principle of the cross. The only quality of life that is going through death and judgment and the fire of God's cleansing and purging, the quality of life which will survive, is the life full of the Holy Spirit—the resurrection life indwelling the child of God and expressed in sacrificial service. The only kind of service which will survive in eternity is service done in the power and unction of the Spirit of God.

The power and the glory of God revealed now in us is something which is going to make heaven lovely. If we would build here on the foundation Jesus Christ, gold, silver, and precious stones—if we build the Christ-life and crucify the flesh—if we build for the glory of God and the honor of Jesus, then some day our testimony is going to make heaven itself all the more beautiful.

". . . the holy Jerusalem, . . . having the glory of God: and her light was like unto a stone most precious. . . . And I saw no temple therein: for the Lord God Almighty and the lamb are the temple of it. And the city had no need of the sun, neither of the moon, to shine in it: for the glory of God did lighten it, and the Lamb is the light thereof. . . . And there shall in no wise enter into it any thing that defileth, neither whatsover worketh abomination, or maketh a lie: but they which are written in the lamb's book of life" (Revelation 21:10–11, 22–23, 27). "For whosoever exalteth himself shall be abased; and he that humbleth himself shall be exalted" (Luke 14:11).

"For *Thine* is the kingdom, and the power and the glory forever!"

Chapter XI

Amen

Martin Luther is quoted as saying that the Lord's prayer is one of the world's greatest martyrs, for it is used so frequently and so thoughtlessly. If that is true of the prayer, I feel it is even more true of the "Amen." That word in prayer has largely lost its significance, yet it is true that as is our "Amen," so has been our prayer.

Let us consider the history of the word. It has always been used as a response in public prayer. It can be found back in the times of Moses and Joshua. When the people of God were assembled in two groups on Mount Ebal and Mount Gerizim, and the principles of blessing and cursing were pronounced, all the people were commanded to say "Amen" (Deuteronomy 27:26). David concluded one of his

140

great psalms of praise by saying, ". . . let all the people say, Amen. Praise ye the Lord!" (Psalm 106: 48). "Amen" has always been the response of the church in prayer, and it would be good to hear it a bit more fervently sometimes than we do.

In the New Testament we find that "Amen" is a name given to the Lord Jesus Christ Himself in the Word of God. To the church at Laodicea He spoke and said, ". . . These things saith the Amen, the faithful and true witness, the beginning of the creation of God" (Revelation 3:14).

When we pray this prayer, therefore, we commence by lifting our hearts to our Father in heaven, and we seal every petition with the name of the Lord Jesus Christ. Now that is a very searching test of our praying, for to pray in the name of the Lord Jesus is not simply to put His name at the end of our prayers, saying, "For Jesus' sake," or "In Jesus' name." That can become a very glib and meaningless phrase. To pray sincerely in His name surely means that we are accepting in our hearts the principles of prayer which He Himself has taught us, and with which this family prayer is surrounded in Matthew 6.

The name of Jesus is not a magic wand, an "open sesame" to all the treasure store of heaven. Certainly it is true that ". . . whatsoever ye shall ask in my name, that will I do . . ." (John 14:13). The Father always gives what the Son asks. But the real test is this: can the Lord Jesus Christ always endorse what *we* ask? Can He present our requests to the throne of heaven? To ask in the name of the Lord Jesus Christ is to be one with Him in desire through the power of the indwelling Holy Spirit. Too often we have the idea that to add the phrase, "In Jesus' name," insures our getting what we want. Do we always stop to ask ourselves if we are really one with Christ in our wishes when we pray?

Writing to the Romans Paul says, ". . . we know not what we should pray for as we ought: but the Spirit itself maketh intercession for us. . . . And he that searcheth the hearts knoweth what is the mind of the Spirit, because he maketh intercession for the saints according to the will of God" (Romans 8:26–27).

To be practical, look at the context in which this family prayer appears, for the pattern of all prayer is set in the context of the principle of all praying, and we must be able to say "Amen" not only to the pattern of prayer but also to the principle.

Take your Bible and glance down the verses of Matthew 6. You will see that in the second verse the Lord Jesus says, ". . . when thou doest thine alms" . . . (or, more literally, "when thou doest righteousness"), and in the fifth verse, ". . . when thou prayest . . . ," and in verse sixteen, ". . . when ye fast. . . . " Alms, prayer, fasting: righteousness, praying, and sacrifice. Observe that we are moving from the outward evidence of our relationship with God to the inward source of all spiritual power. The only proof of a right relationship with God is righteousness of conduct. The power behind righteous conduct is prayer, and the power that makes prayer real and vital—not merely a form—is fasting. That does not mean giving up a meal now and again, but denying everything which interferes with our fellowship with God. When we say "Amen," we are accepting these tremendous principles of prayer.

The Lord Jesus said, "When you do alms, do not sound a trumpet in the street," which is a picture of what a Pharisee would do: sound a silver trumpet to attract the crowd, and then display and distribute his gifts—an ostentatious method of giving, indeed! The Lord was saying that we should not let our giving—or any other righteous conduct—be governed by the opinions of others. We should not give to be recognized nor serve the Lord to be praised of men, but ". . . let not thy left hand know what thy right hand doeth: . . . and thy Father which seeth in secret himself shall reward thee openly" (Matthew 6:3–4). He is concerned only with the motive deep down in our hearts which prompted us to give.

Again He says, "When ye pray do it not to be seen of men." What great instruction for prayer are in verses six and seven: "Shut the door of thy closet . . . and thy Father which seeth in secret shall reward thee openly. . . . Use not vain repetitions." Here we see that prayer should be in privacy, with directness and simplicity. What a contrast to those who make a show of praying with glib phrases and fine terminology! How often do we seek to impress others with the soundness of our doctrine and theology in praying? How much of our praying is out of the passion and love of our hearts? The Lord Jesus said that the

thing which matters in praying is not the publicity
but the privacy.

Again He says, "When you fast, do not be as the
hypocrites who make it obvious they are fasting by
the solemn expression on their faces," in other words,
boasting in public of their sacrifices behind the scenes.
The world should see the joy in your Christian life,
the love and the delight of it: God sees the denial
of yourself and knows what is behind your Christian
life and testimony. Let the world see the joy upon
your face; let the Lord Jesus alone know the price of
it!

Sometimes we meet Christian men and women
whose faces are radiant with the joy of the Lord and
we are tempted to say,"How easy the Christian life
must be for him!" Do we stop to recognize that the
radiance is the result of the fact that behind the
scenes he has renounced himself, and in the depths
of his life there is sacrifice? The Lord Jesus said the
thing that matters concerning our fasting is that it
is secret. We need to remember that if sacrifice and
self-denial in prayer ceases, then prayer ceases to
mean anything, and righteous conduct ceases also.
In each case Christ is drawing the veil aside and
asking us to look deep down into the motives of our
praying, asking us if we can really say "Amen" to
these great principles of prayer.

But notice that "Amen" is also the word of faith
and conviction. When you say "Amen" at the end of
any prayer, and of this prayer in particular, you express the belief that God has absolute power to

answer every petition. God hears prayer, of course—the Bible reveals that—but the blessing of God in answer to our prayer waits upon our asking, unless, of course, there is something deep down in our heart which is an issue between ourselves and our Lord.

At the beginning of our prayer, as was the case with Daniel, the commandment goes forth from the throne and the angels come at His bidding to minister to His children, the heirs of salvation. But they wait until they hear the cry of need and faith. When that has reached the ears of Him who is the hearer and answerer of all prayer, in faithfulness to His promise He sends deliverance. When I say, "Amen," I say it because I believe God is able to do exceeding abundantly above all I can ask or think.

Many of us have reason to know that many times God answers prayer in a different way from what we expect. We have come to Him about some problem, difficulty, or obstacle, and asked Him to remove it, but He has not done that. Instead, He has increased our strength in order to enable us to overcome it. We have asked Him to take away temptation which we feel is too strong to bear, but still it besets us. Has God answered prayer? Indeed He has, for instead of removing it, He has given us purity of heart and victory over the temptation.

Time and time again we have asked Him to break into physical laws and heal the body, yet we have seen some loved one grow weaker and weaker until he has ceased to breathe, and the soul has gone on to be with the Lord. Through all that time of testing

the Word of God has been, ". . . *My* grace is sufficient for thee: for my strength is made perfect in
weakness. . . ." Yes, God has answered prayer. He
has never failed to answer, but frequently He has
answered it in a way that we did not expect.

Sometimes, of course, He gives us more than we
ask. Solomon asked for wisdom, and God gave it to
him, but in addition He gave him riches and a long
life.

We may not always live to see the answer to our
prayer. How many a father and mother have left
behind them children who are right away from God,
though they prayed and agonized for years over the
wayward one who was a heartbreak to them. But
God answered their prayer, and maybe years after
they have gone to be with the Lord the child has been
saved.

Hezekiah, that great man of God, left behind him
a young child of twelve named Manasseh, who was
already showing signs of what we would call juvenile
deliquency. This boy caused his father much heartbreak and inherited his father's throne only to throw
to the winds, apparently, all the good his father had
done. His young life was wasted, but years later he
repented and turned to God.

Sometimes as we go through life praying for this
dear one and that one, God has not answered. We
may keep on praying and believing, and go out into
eternity with a broken heart because the one we love
most of all is utterly careless about the things of

Christ. But God has been testing our patience and faith, and He *has* been answering our prayers.

Paul was converted to the Christian faith after Stephen was martyred, but it was Stephen's prayer, "Lord, lay not this sin to their charge," that was a means of Saul's conversion.

We recognize that when God delays His answer He never denies it, and therefore by faith we seal all our praying with this one word, "Amen." In relation to this family prayer, how wonderful it is to say with conviction, "Amen" to every petition in it! Has not God promised to sanctify His name before all the nations of the world? Therefore His name will be hallowed. Has He not promised to establish His kingdom and to write His law upon our hearts? Therefore His will shall be done. Has He not promised to give us, His people, food and raiment, to pardon our sin, never to allow us to be tempted beyond that we are able to bear? Has He not promised that He will bruise Satan under our feet shortly? Therefore, because we believe Him, because we believe He cannot fail, we acknowledge the power of prayer and seal it by faith with our "Amen."

But when we say, "Amen," in prayer, it is the test of sincerity, the answer of a good conscience. When we pray, do we really want the thing for which we ask? If we do, we will be very careful to obey the commands which accompany every petition.

"Ye ask, and receive not, because ye ask amiss, that ye may consume it upon your lusts" (James 4:3).

Have we recognized that behind every request, every time we go to God in prayer, there is something in relation to that prayer that has to be fulfilled in our lives before He can answer it? For instance, when we pray, "Hallowed be Thy name," and lift our hearts to Him in worship, then comes the command from the throne in heaven, "If that is your prayer, acquaint yourself with God and be at peace"; "Search the Scriptures; for in them . . . ye have eternal life . . ." (John 5:39); "Meditate upon these things; give thyself wholly to them . . ." (I Timothy 4:–15).

We pray, "Thy kingdom come," and the Spirit of God in our hearts says, "If that is your prayer, 'Pray ye therefore the Lord of the harvest, that he will send forth labourers into his harvest'; 'Go ye . . . and preach the gospel to every creature.' " What, in terms of consecration, service, sacrifice, and prayer, are we doing about it? How futile simply to pray these words and leave it at that! God is expecting from every one of His people a response to the "go" as well as to the "pray" and "give."

We pray, "Thy will be done on earth as it is in heaven," and immediately the Spirit of God speaks to the conscience and says, "Submit yourselves to God"; ". . . present your bodies a living sacrifice, holy, acceptable unto God, which is your reasonable service. . . . that ye may prove what is that good, and acceptable, and perfect, will of God" (Romans 12:1–2). ". . . If any man will come after me, let him deny himself, and take up his cross, and follow me" (Matthew 16:24). Have we ever recognized the costliness of praying this prayer and fulfilling it in terms of our personal life?

When our prayer is, "Give us this day our daily bread," the Holy Spirit reminds us, "Be not slothful in business; beware of covetousness, which is idolatry"; "Give, and it shall be given unto you; good measure, pressed down, and shaken together, and running over . . ." (Luke 6:38). These are the precepts which guard our praying. If I pray, "Lord, supply my every need," then I must see to it that I am working to help God answer my prayer.

We pray, "Forgive us our debts," and the Holy Spirit speaks to our conscience and says, "Very well, forgive one another, not once nor seven times, but unto seventy times seven. Love your enemies, do good to them that hate you." If I pray for forgiveness, He expects me to see to it that I am forgiving other people.

When we pray, "Lord Jesus, lead me not into temptation, but deliver me from evil," the Holy Spirit speaks to our conscience, if we utter that prayer in sincerity, saying, "If that is your prayer, 'abhor that which is evil, and cleave to that which is good'; keep yourself unspotted from the world. Resist the devil and he will flee from you. Abide in Christ."

You see, Christian friends, when you really say, "Amen," to the family prayer, it is a test of your sincerity, and when we go through this prayer, each one of its petitions brings an answer from heaven—first of all a precept, and then my obedience, my willingness to accept that, is the channel through which God answers my praying. I am certain that He answers every prayer which is brought to Him in sincerity in the name of the Lord Jesus Christ when we fulfill His conditions.

Perhaps there is another reason why God cannot answer our prayer, also. We may be living, acting, working, and witnessing so that it is impossible for Him to answer. If He sees His children willing to obey His petitions and fulfill His laws in the power of His indwelling Spirit, then He delights to answer. I cannot come with these precious, sacred words on my lips unless I have responded to His demands.

Quite frankly, I do not find prayer to be an easy thing. It is costly if we face it recognizing that obedience is the only channel through which God can answer our prayer. And we cannot in sincerity bring our requests in the name of the Lord Jesus unless deep down in our hearts we see to it we are living a life that makes it possible for God in righteousness to do the thing that we ask of Him.

Are you assenting to the principles of prayer in your life? Are you giving inconspicuously? Are you praying secretly? Are you sacrificing privately? ". . . and thy Father which seeth in secret shall reward thee openly" (Matthew 6:6).

Are you acknowledging the power of prayer? Do you put "Amen" to this and every prayer in the absolute, unshakable conviction that God hears and answers, even though it may be in a way that you do not expect or at some distant time?

Are you accepting His precepts in your living? It

would revolutionize our prayer life as church members and as individuals if we recognized that sometimes we make it impossible for God to answer our petitions because our praying is not supported by our obedience.

When you pray the family prayer ask yourself, "Is His name hallowed in my life? Is God having His will and way with me? Am I diligent in my daily work? Am I forgiving? Am I abhorring all that is evil and cleaving to that which is good?

"Am I making it possible for God to answer my prayers—to answer, most of all, this prayer?"

Our Father which art in heaven,
Hallowed be thy name.
Thy kingdom come. Thy will be done
In earth, as it is in heaven.

Give us this day our daily bread.
And forgive us our debts, as we forgive
our debtors.
And lead us not into temptation,
But deliver us from evil:

For thine is the kingdom,
And the power, and the glory, for ever.

Amen.